ENGLISH GRAMMAR FOR STUDENTS OF FRENCH

The Study Guide for Those Learning French

Second edition

by
Jacqueline Morton

The Olivia and Hill Press®

English Grammar series
  edited by Jacqueline Morton

English Grammar for Students of French, 2nd edition
English Grammar for Students of Spanish, 2nd edition
English Grammar for Students of German, 2nd edition
English Grammar for Students of Italian
English Grammar for Students of Latin
English Grammar for Students of Russian

Printed in the U.S.A.

Library of Congress Catalog Card Number: 87-7889

ISBN 0-934034-09-5

10 9 8 7 6 5 4 3

Contents

To the Student

English Grammar for Students of French is a handbook that will help you get the most out of your French textbook as well as answer some of the questions you might be reluctant to ask in class.

Most teachers incorporate **English Grammar** into the Class Syllabus so you will know which pages to read before doing an assignment in your French textbook. If you have to select the pages yourself, check the index to find where the grammatical terms and concepts you will be studying in the textbook are covered in this handbook.

How to Use the **English Grammar** Handbook

- Read carefully, making sure you understand the explanations and the examples.
- Do the **Practice** at the end of the chapter you have read.
- Compare your answers with the Answer Key at the end of the handbook. If they don't match, review the section.

Now you are ready to do your assignment in your textbook.

Tips for Studying a Foreign Language

1. **Rules**—Make sure you understand each rule before you move on to the next one. Language learning is like building a house; each brick is only as secure as its foundation.

2. **Memorization**—Memorization plays an important part in language learning. For instance, you will have to memorize vocabulary, verb conjugations, and grammar rules. Here are the steps you should follow in memorizing verb conjugations and rules.

- Divide the passage to be memorized into sections you can easily remember (for instance, 2 sentences).
- Read the first section aloud several times.
- Write down the first section as you repeat it aloud to yourself.
- Compare what you wrote with the original.

- Repeat the last 2 steps until there is no difference between what you said or wrote and the original.
- Repeat these steps to memorize the second section.
- Continue memorizing each section in the same way, reciting from the beginning each time.

3. **Vocabulary**—Use any trick or gimmick that helps you remember. Here are some that students have found useful:

- Write each word on a separate index card, French on one side, English on the other.
- Use index cards or pens of different colors. This can help you remember other useful information about the word: using blue for masculine nouns and pink for feminine nouns will help you remember genders. (You can also use green for verbs, orange for adjectives, etc. to remember parts of speech).
- When learning the French words, look at the English words. Say the French word that corresponds aloud, and flip the card to check your answer. Shuffle the deck often so you see the English word cold (i.e., without remembering the word order).

4. **Written exercises**—Read the French words and sentences out loud as you write them. That way you are practicing seeing, saying and hearing the words. It will help you remember them.

5. **Daily practice**—Don't get behind. It's almost impossible to catch up in language learning because you need daily practice and time to absorb the material.

6. **Language laboratory**—It is better to listen to tapes for short periods several times during the week rather than doing everything in one long session.

Bonne chance,

Jacqueline Morton

Introduction

When you learn a foreign language, in this case French, you must look at each word in three ways:

1. The **meaning** of the word—the English word must be connected with a French word that has an equivalent meaning.

   Boy, a young male child, has the same meaning as the French word **garçon.**

Words with equivalent meanings are learned by memorizing **vocabulary** items. Sometimes two words are the same or very similar in both English and French. These words are called **cognates** and are, of course, easy to learn.

FRENCH	ENGLISH
intelligent	intelligent
gouvernement	government
continuer	continue

Occasionally knowing one French word will help you learn another.

   Knowing that **étudiant** is a *male student* should help you learn that **étudiante** is a *female student;* or knowing that **vendeur** is a *salesman* should help you remember that **vendeuse** is a *saleswoman.*

Usually there is little similarity between words, and knowing one French word will not help you learn another. As a general rule, you must memorize each vocabulary item separately.

   Knowing that **garçon** is *boy* will not help you learn that **fille** is *girl.*

In addition, there are times when words in combination take on a special meaning.

> The French word **faire** means *to make;* **la queue** means *the tail.* However, **faire la queue** means *to line up, to stand in line.*

An expression whose meaning as a whole (**faire la queue**) is different from the meaning of the individual words (**faire** and **la queue**) is called an **idiom.** You will need to pay special attention to these idiomatic expressions in order to recognize them and use them correctly.

2. The **classification** of the word—English and French words are classified in eight categories called **parts of speech.** Here is a list of the parts of speech used in French:

noun	article
verb	adverb
pronoun	preposition
adjective	conjunction

Each part of speech has its own rules for spelling, pronunciation, and use. You must learn to recognize what part of speech a word is in order to choose the correct French equivalent and know what rules to apply.

Look at the word *what* in the following sentences:

> a. *What* do you want?
> b. *What* movie do you want to see?
> c. I'll do *what* you want.[1]

The English word is the same in all three sentences; but in French three different words will be used and three different sets of rules will apply because each *what* belongs to a different part of speech.

---

[1]a. Interrogative pronoun, see p. 171.
  b. Interrogative adjective, see p. 127.
  c. Relative pronoun without antecedent, see p. 208.

3. The **use** of the word—a word must also be identified according to the role it plays in the sentence. Each word, whether English or French, plays a specific role. Determining this role or **function** will also help you to choose the correct French equivalent and to know what rules to apply.

Let us go back again to the word *what*. Examine its function in the following sentences:

    a. *What* is on the table?
    b. *What* is she doing?
    c. *What* are you talking about?[1]

Because *what* has a different function in each sentence above, its French equivalent will be different in each sentence.

As a student of French you must learn to recognize both the part of speech and the function of each word in a given sentence. This is essential because words in a French sentence have a great deal of influence on one another.

*The small black **shoes** are on the big round table.*

Les petites **chaussures** noires sont sur la grande **table** ronde.

In English: The only word that affects another word in the sentence is *shoes,* which forces us to say *are.* If the word were *shoe,* we would have to say *is.*

In French: The word for *shoes* (**chaussures**) not only affects the word for *are* (**sont**), but also the spelling and pronunciation of the French words for *the, small,* and *black.* The word for *table* (**table**) affects the spelling and pronunciation of the French words for *the, big,* and *round.* The only word not affected by another word is **sur,** which means *on.*

---

[1]a. Subject, see p. 174.
b. Direct object, see p. 174.
c. Object of a preposition, see p. 175.

Since parts of speech and function are usually determined in the same way in English and in French, this handbook will show you how to identify them in English. You will then learn to compare English and French constructions. This will give you a better understanding of the explanations in your French grammar book.

What is a Noun?

A **noun** is a word that can be the name of a person, an animal, place, thing, event, or an idea.

In English: Let us look at some different types of words which are nouns:

a person	professor, clown, student, girl Professor Smith, Bozo, Paul, Mary
an animal	dog, bird, bear, snake Heidi, Tweetie, Teddy
a place	city, state, country, continent Paris, Michigan, France, Europe
a thing	lamp, airplane, book, dress Mona Lisa, Eiffel Tower, Arch of Triumph
an event or activity	graduation, marriage, birth, death, football robbery, rest, growth
an idea or concept	poverty, democracy, humor, mathematics addition, strength, elegance, virtue, increase

As you can see, a noun is not only a word which names something that is tangible, i.e., that you can touch, such as *table, dog,* and *White House,* etc., it can also be the name of things that are abstract, i.e., that you cannot touch, such as *justice, jealousy,* and *honor.*

A noun that does not state the name of a specific person, place, thing, etc. is called a **common noun**. A common noun does not begin with a capital letter, unless it is the first word of a sentence. All the words above that are not capitalized are common nouns.

A noun that is the name of a specific person, place, thing, etc. is called a **proper noun**. A proper noun always begins with a capital letter. All the words above that are capitalized are proper nouns.

> The girl is Mary.
> | |
> common proper
> noun   noun

A noun that is made up of two words is called a **compound noun**. A compound noun can be a common noun, such as *comic strip* and *ice cream,* or a proper noun, such as *Western Europe* and *North America.*

To help you learn to recognize nouns, look at the paragraph below where the nouns are in *italics.*

> The best *purchases* from *France* include *wines, perfumes, scarves, gloves* and other luxury *items.* Today, French *workers* make excellent *skis* and *tennis rackets* which are sold the *world* over. Thanks to the *Common Market,* you can find *goods* from *Germany, Italy, England,* and their commercial *partners* in all large French *stores.* Thus, Italian *sportscars,* English *leather,* German *glassware,* and Belgian *lace* can be bought at *prices* comparable to those in the *country* of *origin.*

In French: Nouns are identified in the same way they are in English.

TERMS USED TO TALK ABOUT NOUNS

• A noun has a gender; that is, it can be classified according to whether it is masculine, feminine, or neuter (see **What is Meant by Gender?,** p. 7).

- A noun has a number; that is, it can be identified according to whether it is singular or plural (see **What is Meant by Number?,** p. 12).

- A noun can have a variety of functions in a sentence; that is, it can be the subject of the sentence (see **What is a Subject?,** p. 40) or an object (see **What are Objects?,** p. 148).

Practice

Circle the nouns in the following sentences:

1. The boy came into the classroom and spoke to the teacher.

2. The Smiths went to France by ship.

3. The textbook has a painting on its cover.

4. Mary Evans visited Paris with her class.

5. The temperature in the classroom was very high.

6. The lion roared and the children screamed.

7. Truth is stranger than fiction.

8. His kindness and understanding were known throughout the world.

9. Honesty is the best policy.

What is Meant by Gender?

When a word can be classified as masculine, feminine, or neuter, it is said to have **gender.**

Gender is not very important in English; however, it is at the very heart of the French language where the gender of a word is often reflected in the way the word is spelled and pronounced. More parts of speech have a gender in French than in English. Parts of speech that indicate gender:

ENGLISH	FRENCH
pronouns	nouns
possessive adjectives	pronouns
	articles
	adjectives

Since each part of speech follows its own rules to indicate gender, you will find this discussed in the sections dealing with articles and the various types of pronouns and adjectives. In this section we shall only look at the gender of nouns.

In English: Nouns themselves do not have a gender, but sometimes their meaning will indicate a gender based on the biological sex of the person or animal the noun stands for. When we replace a proper or common noun with *he* or *she,* we automatically use *he* for males and *she* for females. All the nouns which name things that do not have a sex are replaced by *it.*

Nouns referring to males indicate the **masculine** gender.

> Paul came home; *he* was tired, and I was glad to see *him.*
> noun   masculine   masculine
> male

Nouns referring to females indicate the **feminine** gender.

> The girl came home; *she* was tired, and I was glad to see *her.*
> noun   feminine   feminine
> female

All other nouns do not indicate a gender; they are considered **neuter.**

The city of Washington is lovely. I enjoyed visiting *it*.[1]
    | |
  noun   neuter

In French: All nouns—common nouns and proper nouns—are either masculine or feminine. There is no such thing as a noun without a gender.

The **biological gender** is the gender of nouns whose meaning is always tied to one or the other of the biological sexes, male or female. The gender of these nouns is easy to determine.

MALES = MASCULINE	FEMALES = FEMININE
Paul	Mary
boy	girl
brother	sister
stepfather	aunt

You must make sure, however, that the noun can refer only to one sex or another. For instance, "father" can only be a male; therefore, the French noun for "father" is of the masculine gender. The noun "professor," however, can refer to a female or male. Therefore, the meaning of the noun itself will not reveal its gender.

The gender of all other nouns, common and proper, cannot be explained or figured out. These nouns have a **grammatical gender** which is unrelated to biological sex.

EXAMPLES OF ENGLISH NOUNS WHOSE EQUIVALENTS ARE *MASCULINE* IN FRENCH	EXAMPLES OF ENGLISH NOUNS WHOSE EQUIVALENTS ARE *FEMININE* IN FRENCH
boat	car
suicide	library
book	virtue

---

[1]There are a few well-known exceptions, such as *ship*, which is referred to as *she*. It is custom, not logic, which decides.

The S/S United States sailed for Europe. *She* is a beautiful ship.

vice	death
Japan	France
murder	strength
vice	democracy
paradise	power
professor	birth

You will have to memorize the grammatical gender of every French noun you learn. This gender is important not only for the noun itself, but for the spelling and pronunciation of the words it influences.

ENDINGS INDICATING GENDER

Gender can sometimes be determined by looking at the end of the French noun. Below are some endings that are often found in masculine nouns and others that are usually found in feminine nouns. Since you will encounter many nouns with these endings in basic French, it is certainly worthwhile to familiarize yourself with them.[1]

MASCULINE ENDINGS

-age	village, potage, collage
-al	journal, animal, hôpital
-at	chocolat, consulat, baccalauréat
-eau	tableau, chapeau, bateau
-ent	président, client, patient
-er	déjeuner, dîner, souper
	menuisier, boulanger, boucher (*trades*)
	poirier, oranger, pommier (*trees*)
-et	objet, sujet, projet
-eur	vendeur, porteur, chanteur (*trades*)
	moteur, radiateur, calculateur (*devices*)
-ien	mécanicien, pharmacien, politicien
-in	cousin, voisin, médecin
-isme	communisme, nationalisme, optimisme
-oir	devoir, couloir, soir
-ment	gouvernement, appartement, monument

---

[1] We thank Professor Michio Hagiwara and his publisher for authorization to reproduce this list from *Thème et Variations* (New York: John Wiley & Sons), 1977.

FEMININE ENDINGS

-ade	salade, marmelade, façade
-aine	fontaine, chaîne, laine
-aison	conjugaison, terminaison, maison
-ance	correspondance, dance, France
-ande	commande, demande, viande
-ée	soirée, journée, entrée
-eille	oreille, bouteille, corbeille
-ence	agence, présence, absence
-ère	boulangère, bouchère, ménagère (*trades*)
-esse	maîtresse, hôtesse, politesse
-ette	fourchette, assiette, serviette
-euse	vendeuse, chanteuse, danseuse
-ie	économie, géographie, compagnie
-ienne	comédienne, musicienne, canadienne
-ine	cousine, voisine, médecine
-ique	technique, musique, panique
-ise	valise, surprise, église
-oire	poire, victoire, histoire
-onne	personne, Sorbonne, bonne
-sion	télévision, mission, profession
-té	liberté, nationalité, bonté
-tion	question, nation, addition
-trice	actrice, directrice, monitrice
-tude	étude, solitude, attitude
-ure	voiture, culture, architecture

Practice

I. The French gender of some English nouns is obvious; for others you will have to consult a dictionary. Look at the list below.
- Write *masculine* or *feminine* next to the nouns whose gender you can identify.
- Write "?" next to the nouns whose gender you would have to look up.

GENDER IN FRENCH

1. boys   _____

2. chair   _____

3. Jane   _____

4. uncles   _____

5. visitor   _____

6. sisters   _____

7. houses   _____

II. By consulting the list on pp. 9–10, establish the gender of the following French words.

GENDER

1. vérité   _____

2. division   _____

3. cadeau   _____

4. ordinateur   _____

5. biologie   _____

What is Meant by Number?

Number in the grammatical sense means the word is singular or plural. When a word refers to one person or thing, it is said to be **singular;** when it refers to more than one, it is **plural.**

More parts of speech indicate number in French, and there are more spelling and pronunciation changes in French than in English. Parts of speech that indicate number:

ENGLISH	FRENCH
nouns	nouns
verbs	verbs
pronouns	pronouns
only demonstrative	adjectives
adjectives	articles

Since each part of speech follows its own rules to indicate number, you will find this discussed in the sections dealing with articles, the various types of adjectives and pronouns, as well as in all the sections on verbs and their tenses. In this section we shall only look at the number of nouns.

In English: A singular noun is made plural in a couple of ways:

- by adding "-*s*" or "-*es*" to the singular noun

book	books
kiss	kisses

- by making a spelling change

man	men
mouse	mice
leaf	leaves
child	children

A plural noun is usually spelled and pronounced differently from the singular.

Some nouns, called **collective nouns,** refer to a group of persons or things, but the noun itself is considered singular.

> A football *team* has eleven players.
> The *family* is well.
> The *crowd* was under control.

In French: As in English, the plural form of a noun is usually spelled differently from the singular. The most common change is the same one made in English; that is, an "**-s**" is added to the singular noun.

livre	livres
table	tables

Hearing the Plural

The main difference between the plural forms in the two languages is that in French, even though you can see the plural ending if you are reading the word, you can rarely hear it, because the final "s" is never pronounced.

same pronunciation

livre	livres
table	tables

You have to listen to the word that comes before the noun to know whether the noun is singular or plural. The examples below show you that in English you hear the plural in the noun itself, while in French you hear it in the word that precedes it.

	SINGULAR	PLURAL
ENGLISH	the **book**	the **books**
	the **table**	the **tables**
FRENCH	**le** livre	**les** livres
	la table	**les** tables

-**AL** WORDS

There is an important group of French words that end in -**al** in the singular and which change to -**aux** in the plural.

SINGULAR
le journ**al** *newspaper*
l'anim**al**   *animal*

PLURAL
les journ**aux** *newspapers*
les anim**aux** *animals*

In this group of words you can hear the plural in the noun itself as well as in the word that precedes it.

Note: Nouns do not change gender when they become plural.

Practice

The following is a list of English and French words.
- Look at the words.
  Under COLUMN A circle (S) or (P), depending on whether the word is singular or plural.
- Say the words aloud.
  Under COLUMN B circle (S) or (P) if you can hear that the word is singular or plural. Circle (?) if you can't tell whether it is singular or plural.

	COLUMN A		COLUMN B		
1. desks	S	P	S	P	?
2. **maisons**	S	P	S	P	?
3. apartment	S	P	S	P	?
4. samples	S	P	S	P	?
5. **étudiantes**	S	P	S	P	?
6. tooth	S	P	S	P	?

7. **cheval**	S	P	S	P	?
8. feet	S	P	S	P	?
9. **canaux**	S	P	S	P	?
10. group	S	P	S	P	?

What are Articles?

An **article** is a word placed before a noun to show whether the noun refers to a particular person, animal, place, thing, event, or idea, or whether the noun refers to an unspecified person, thing, or idea.

In English: Let us look at the two types of articles.

1. A **definite article** is used before a noun when we are speaking about a particular person, place, animal, thing, or idea. There is one definite article, *the.*

    I saw *the* boy you spoke to me about.
        |
        a particular boy

    I ate *the* apple you gave me.
        |
        a particular apple

The definite article remains *the* when the noun which follows becomes plural.

    I saw *the boys* you spoke to me about.
    I ate *the apples* you gave me.

2. An **indefinite article** is used before a noun when we are speaking about an unspecified person, animal, place, thing, event, or idea. There are two indefinite articles, *a* and ***an.***

A is used before a word beginning with a consonant.[1]

> I saw *a* boy in the street.
> |
> not a particular boy

An is used before a word beginning with a vowel.

> I ate *an* apple.
> |
> not a particular apple

The indefinite article is used only with a singular noun; it is dropped when the noun becomes plural. At times, the word *some* is used to replace it.

> I saw boys in the street.
> I saw *some* boys in the street.

> I ate apples.
> I ate *some* apples.

In French: You will have to pay much more attention to French definite and indefinite articles than you do to their English equivalents. In French the article works hand in hand with the noun it belongs to in that it matches the noun's gender and number. This "matching" is called **agreement.** (One says that "the article agrees with the noun.") A different article is used depending on whether the noun is masculine or feminine, and depending on whether the noun is singular or plural. Because these articles are both pronounced and spelled differently, they indicate the gender and number of the noun to the ear as well as to the eye.

---

[1]Vowels are the sounds associated with the letters *a, e, i, o* and *u;* consonants are the sounds associated with the other letters of the alphabet.

1. There are four forms of the definite article.

Le indicates that the noun is masculine singular.

le livre	*the book*
le garçon	*the boy*

La indicates that the noun is feminine singular.

la table	*the table*
la pomme	*the apple*

L' is used instead of **le** and **la** before a word beginning with a vowel. The dropping of a final vowel before a word starting with a vowel is called an **elision.** You will have to rely on the dictionary or your memory to know if the word is masculine or feminine.

l'étudiant   *the student*
  |
masculine

l'école   *the school*
  |
feminine

Les indicates that the noun is plural; it does not tell you the gender because **les** is used with both masculine and feminine plural nouns.

MASCULINE PLURAL
les livres	*the books*
les garçons	*the boys*

FEMININE PLURAL
les tables	*the tables*
les pommes	*the apples*

In written French, you can see the plural form in both the definite article **les** and in the nouns *livres, garçons, tables,* and *pommes.*

Although it is easy to see the difference between **le** and **la**, it is harder to hear the difference because the masculine **le** often sounds like an "l" attached to the previous word.

Voilà le livre. (pronounced: "Voilal" livre.)

It is easier, therefore, to listen for the feminine article **la**, because the "a" is generally not dropped in pronunciation. If you hear the "a," you know that the noun that follows is feminine; if you don't hear the "a," assume that the article is **le** and that the noun following is masculine.

In spoken French, you will hear the plural form differently depending on whether the noun begins with a consonant or a vowel.

- If the noun begins with a consonant, you will hear the plural only in the definite article **les** (sounds like "lay") that comes before the noun, since the "s" at the end of the plural noun is not pronounced.

> **les** tables
> |
> "lay"

- If the noun begins with a vowel, you will hear the plural twice; first, you will hear the **les,** and then you will hear a "z" sound when the final consonant of **les** is linked to the beginning vowel of the noun.

> **les** étudiants
> └┬┘
> "layzay"

The linking of a final consonant to a word that follows and begins with a vowel is called a **liaison.**

2. There are three forms of the indefinite article.

   Un indicates that the noun is masculine singular.

un livre	*a book*
un garçon	*a boy*

   Une indicates that the noun is feminine singular.

une table	*a table*
une pomme	*an apple*

   Des indicates that the noun is plural; it does not tell you the gender because **des** is used with both masculine and feminine plural nouns.

   MASCULINE PLURAL

des livres	*books*
des garçons	*boys*

   FEMININE PLURAL

des tables	*tables*
des pommes	*apples*

   Here again, you will have no problem in recognizing the plural form when you read these words; however, you will be able to hear the plural forms only in the plural indefinite article **des** (sounds like "day") preceding the noun (and in the *liaison* if the noun starts with a vowel).

   Memorize French nouns with their singular indefinite articles. These articles do not change when they are followed by a vowel and will always tell you if the noun is masculine or feminine.

3. French also has another set of articles called **partitive articles** because they refer to *"part* of the whole." They are used before certain singular nouns and correspond to *some* or *any* in English.

Notice that even when *some* or *any* is not expressed in the English sentence, the partitive must be used in the French sentence.

Du indicates that the noun is masculine singular.

> Je mange **du** pain.
> *I am eating (**some**) bread.*

> Avez-vous **du** pain?
> *Do you have (**any**) bread?*

De la indicates that the noun is feminine singular.

> J'achète **de la** viande.
> *I am buying (**some**) meat.*

> Voulez-vous **de la** confiture?
> *Do you want (**any**) jam?*

De l' is used instead of **du** and **de la** before a word beginning with a vowel. It therefore does not tell us if the noun is masculine or feminine, just that it is singular.

> Je bois **de l'**eau.
> |
>   feminine

> *I am drinking (**some**) water.*

> Devez-vous **de l'**argent à Mary?
> |
>   masculine

> *Do you owe (**any**) money to Mary?*

This is just a brief summary of the different forms of the partitive articles. Refer to your textbook for the rules regarding their usage.

Practice

The following is a list of English nouns preceded by definite and indefinite articles. The French DICTIONARY ENTRY shows you if the noun (n.) is masculine (m.) or feminine (f.).

• Write the French article for each noun in the space provided.

	DICTIONARY ENTRY	FRENCH
1. **the** books	livre (n.m.)	_____
2. **the** friend	ami (n.m.)	_____
3. **some** chairs	chaise (n.f.)	_____
4. **an** idea	idée (n.f.)	_____
5. **some** money	argent (n.m.)	_____
6. **the** table	table (n.f.)	_____
7. **a** course	cours (n.m.)	_____
8. **some** bread	pain (n.m.)	_____
9. **the** dinner	dîner (n.m.)	_____
10. **some** ice-cream	glace (n.f.)	_____

What is a Mute "h"?

In English: An "h" that is not pronounced is called a **mute "h."** Compare your pronunciation of the following words that begin with the letter "h":

COLUMN 1	COLUMN 2
hotel	hour
horse	honor
hat	heir

The "h" is pronounced in the words in Column 1, whereas the "h" is silent in the words in Column 2. The words in Column 2, therefore, start with a mute "h."

The indefinite article *an* (instead of *a*) is used before a word starting with a mute "h."

a hotel	an hour
a horse	an honor
a hat	an heir

In French: The letter "h" exists only in writing. It is never pronounced. However, it falls into two categories depending on how it affects spelling and pronunciation.

1. The **"h" muet** (mute h) is the most common. The "h" is ignored and the word is considered as beginning with a vowel.

    un hôtel   une herbe

There are two important consequences:

In the singular, there is an elision; **le** and **la** change to **l'**. (See p. 17.)

    l'hôtel   l'herbe

In the plural, there is a *liaison;* the final "s" of **les** or **des** is linked in pronunciation with the vowel that follows, giving a "z" sound.

    les hôtels   **les her**bes
      "layzo"   "layzayr"

2. The **"h" aspiré** (aspirate "h") is rare. The "h" is considered an unpronounced consonant.

There are two important consequences:

In the singular, there is no elision.

    le héros[1]   *the hero*
    la hâte   *the haste*

In the plural, there is no *liaison*.

        les héros[1]
         ⌞⌝
        "layay"

There are not many words that start with an aspirate "h." They are usually identified in dictionaries with a dot under the "h" or with an asterisk in front of the word.

Practice

The following are the dictionary entries of French words beginning with the letter "h."

• Fill in the appropriate French definite article in the space provided.

1. hôtel (n.m.)   _____ hôtel

2. *hauteur (n.f.)   _____ hauteur

3. hôpital (n.m.)   _____ hôpital

4. *héros (n.m.)   _____ héros

5. homme (n.m.)   _____ homme

---

[1]The French word for heroine does not start with an aspirate "h"; therefore, its singular is **l'héroine** and its plural is **les héroines** with a *liaison*.
        ⌞⌝
      "layzay"

What is the Possessive?

The term **possessive** means that one noun owns or *possesses* another noun.

In English: You can show possession in one of two ways.

1. An *apostrophe* can be used.

    • an apostrophe + "s" is added to a singular possessor

> Mary's dress
> |
> singular possessor

> Verlaine's poetry
> the professor's book
> a tree's branches
> the lady's handbag

    • an apostrophe is added to a plural possessor

> the students' teacher
> |
> plural possessor

> the girls' club

2. The word *of* can be used.

    • *of* is placed before a proper noun possessor

> the dress *of* Mary
> |
> proper noun possessor

> the poetry *of* Verlaine

- *of the* or *of a,* is placed before a singular or plural common noun possessor

> the book *of the* professor
> |
> singular common noun possessor

> the branches *of a* tree
> the handbag *of the* lady
> the teacher *of the* students
> |
> plural common noun possessor

In French: There is only one way to express possession and that is by using the "of" construction (2 above). The apostrophe structure does not exist. When you want to show possession in French you must change an English structure using an apostrophe to a structure using *of* (**de**).

Mary's dress	the dress *of Mary* la robe **de** Marie
the professor's book	the book **of the** professor le livre **du** professeur de + le
a tree's branches	the branches **of a** tree les branches **d'un** arbre
the lady's handbag	the handbag **of the** lady le sac **de la** dame
the students' teacher	the teacher **of the** students le professeur **des** étudiants de + les

Note: Do not confuse **du, de la, de l'** and **des** meaning *of* and *of the* with words of the same spelling which are partitive articles (see p. 19) and the plural indefinite article (p. 19) meaning *some* or *any*. When they indicate possession, they usually come between two nouns (*the book* of the *teacher*).

Practice

The following are possessives using the apostrophe.
 • Write the alternate English structure which is the word-for-word
   equivalent of the French structure.

1. some children's parents

_____

2. the dress's color

_____

3. the school's entrance

_____

4. a car's speed

_____

5. the books' covers

_____

What is a Verb?

A **verb** is a word that indicates "the action" of the sentence. The word
"action" is used in its broadest sense, not necessarily physical action.

In English: Let us look at different types of words which are verbs:

a physical activity	to run, to hit, to talk, to walk, to box
a mental activity	to hope, to believe, to imagine, to dream, to think
a condition	to be, to sit, to have

Many verbs, however, do not fall neatly into one of the above categories. They are verbs nevertheless because they represent the "action" of the sentence.

The book *costs* only $5.00.
| to cost

The students *seem* tired.
| to seem

To help you learn to recognize verbs, look at the paragraph below where the verbs are in *italics*.

The three students *entered* the restaurant, *selected* a table, *hung* up their coats and *sat* down. They *looked* at the menu and *asked* the waitress what she *recommended*. She *advised* the daily special, beef stew. It *was* not expensive. They *chose* a bottle of red wine and *ordered* a salad. The service *was* slow, but the food *tasted* very good. Good cooking, they *decided, takes* time. They *ate* pastry for dessert and *finished* the meal with coffee.

The verb is one of the most important words in a sentence; you cannot express a complete thought (i.e., write a **complete sentence**) without a verb. It is important that you learn to identify verbs because the function of many words in a sentence often depends on their relationship to the verb. For instance, the subject of a sentence is the word doing the action of the verb, and the object is the word receiving the action of the verb (see **What is a Subject?**, p. 40, and **What are Objects?**, p. 148).

There are two types of verbs in both English and French, transitive and intransitive.

1. A **transitive verb** is a verb which takes a direct object (see **What are Objects?**, p. 148). It is indicated by the abbreviation *v.t.* (verb transitive) in dictionaries.

The boy *threw* the ball.
       | |
   transitive direct object

She *quit* her job.
   | |
 transitive direct object

2. An **intransitive verb** is a verb that does not take a direct object. It is indicated by the abbreviation *v.i.* (verb intransitive) in the dictionary.

Paul *is sleeping*.
     |
   intransitive

She *will arrive* soon.
    | |
 intransitive   adverb

Many verbs can be used transitively or intransitively in sentences, depending on whether they have a direct object or not.

The students *speak* French.
     | |
  transitive direct object

Actions *speak* louder than words.
    |
  intransitive

In English it is possible to change the meaning of a verb by placing short words (prepositions or adverbs) after them. The verb *look* in Column A changes meaning depending on the word that follows it:

COLUMN A		COLUMN B
to look *for*	=	to search for I am looking for a book.
to look *after*	=	to take care of I am looking after the children.
to look *out*	=	to beware of Look out for lions.

to look *into*	=	to investigate
		I am looking into it.
to look *over*	=	to check
		I am looking over my exam.

In French: Verbs are identified the same way that they are in English. However, be careful of the following two pitfalls:

1. Some verbs that are transitive in English are intransitive in French, while other verbs that are intransitive in English are transitive in French. Examples of these verbs are given in the section **What are Objects?**, p. 148.

2. It is impossible to change the meaning of a verb by adding short words as in Column A above. In French, you would have to use an entirely different verb in each of the above sentences. When looking up verbs in the dictionary, be sure to look for the specific meaning under the dictionary entry. For instance, all the examples above under Column A will be found under the dictionary entry *look,* but you will have to search for the expression *look for* or *look after* to find the correct French equivalent. Don't select the first entry under *look* and then add on the French equivalent for *after;* the result will be meaningless in French.

TERMS USED TO TALK ABOUT VERBS

• The verb form which is the name of the verb is called an infinitive: *to eat, to sleep, to drink* (see **What is an Infinitive?**, p. 30).

• A verb is conjugated or changes in form to agree with its subject: *I do, he does* (see **What is a Verb Conjugation?**, p. 51).

• A verb indicates tense, that is, the time (present, past, or future) of the action: *I am, I was, I will be* (see **What is Meant by Tense?**, p. 69).

• A verb shows voice, that is, the relation between the subject and the action of the verb (see **What is Meant by Active and Passive Voice?**, p. 107).

- A verb shows mood, that is, the speakers' attitude toward what they are saying (see **What is Meant by Mood?**, p. 67).

- A verb may also be used to form a participle (see **What is a Participle?**, p. 76).

Practice

Circle the verbs in the following sentences.

1. The students purchase their lunch at school.
2. Paul and Mary were happy.
3. They enjoyed the movie, but they preferred the book.
4. Paul ate dinner, finished his novel, and then went to bed.
5. Mary suddenly realized that she dreamt every night.
6. The teacher felt sick yesterday, but today she seems fine.
7. The anxious parents stayed home because they expected a phone call.
8. It was sad to see the little dog struggle to get out of the lake.
9. I attended a concert to celebrate the new year.
10. The price of food increases, but my salary remains the same.

What is an Infinitive?

An **infinitive** is the name of the verb. It is under the infinitive form that you will find a verb in the dictionary.

In English: The infinitive is composed of two words: *to* + the dictionary form of the verb (*to speak, to dance*). By **dictionary form,** we mean the form of the verb that is listed as the entry in the dictionary (*speak, dance*). Although the infinitive is the most basic form of the verb, it can never be used in a sentence without another verb.

To learn is exciting.
infinitive main verb

It'*s* (it *is*) important *to be* on time.
main verb   infinitive

Paul and Mary *want to dance* together.
              main verb infinitive

It *has started to rain.*
   auxiliary main infinitive
       verb

The dictionary form of the verb, i.e., the infinitive without the *to,* is used after such verbs as *must* and *let.*

Paul *must do* his homework.
      infinitive

The parents *let* the children *see* the presents.
                              infinitive

In French: The infinitive form is shown by the last two or three letters of the verb called **the ending;** the English word *to* in the infinitive has no French equivalent.

dans**er**	*to dance*
fin**ir**	*to finish*
vend**re**	*to sell*

These endings, called **la terminaison** in French, also tell you which group each verb belongs to:

-er verbs belong to the 1st group
-ir verbs belong to the 2nd group
-re verbs belong to the 3rd group

It is important for you to identify the group to which a verb belongs so you will know what pattern to follow in conjugating that verb (see **What is a Verb Conjugation?**, p. 51).

In a sentence, the infinitive form is always used for a verb that depends on another verb which is neither **avoir** (*to have*) nor **être** (*to be*).

> *Paul and Mary want **to speak** French.*
> Paul et Marie *veulent* **parler** français.
>   1st verb infinitive

> *Paul and Mary can **leave** if they wish.*
> Paul et Marie *peuvent* **partir** s'ils désirent.
>   1st verb infinitive

> *You must **take** the books to school.*
> Tu *dois* **prendre** les livres à l'école.
>   1st verb   infinitive

Notice that in the last two examples there is no "to" in the English sentence to alert you that an infinitive must be used in French.

Practice

I. Under what word would you look up these verbs in the dictionary?

DICTIONARY FORM

1. Mary *wrote* that book in France.   _____

2. Paul *swam* regularly.   _____

3. I *am* tired today.   _____

4. The children *spoke* French well.   _____

5. They *had* a cold.   _____

6. He *taught* them everything he knew.   _____

II. Circle the words that you would replace with an infinitive in French.

1. Mary has nothing more to do today.

2. The students must study their lessons.

3. Paul wants to learn French.

4. They can leave on Tuesday.

5. Paul and Mary hope to travel this summer.

What are Auxiliary Verbs?

A verb is called an **auxiliary verb** or **helping verb** when it helps another verb form one of its tenses (see **What is Meant by Tense?**, p. 69). When it is used alone, it functions as a main verb.

Mary *is* a girl.	*is*	MAIN VERB
Paul *has* a headache.	*has*	MAIN VERB
They *go* to the movies.	*go*	MAIN VERB
They ***have*** gone to the movies.	***have***	AUXILIARY VERB
	gone	MAIN VERB
He ***has been*** gone two weeks.	***has***	AUXILIARY VERB
	been	AUXILIARY VERB
	gone	MAIN VERB

In English: There are many auxiliary verbs, for example, *to have, to be,* and *to do.* They have two primary uses:

1. to indicate the tense of the main verb (present, past, future—see **What is Meant by Tense?**, p. 69)

Mary *is* reading a book.	PRESENT
Mary *was* reading a book.	PAST
Mary *will* read a book.	FUTURE

2. to help formulate questions

Bob *has* a dog.	*has*	MAIN VERB
Does Bob *have* a dog?	*does*	AUXILIARY VERB
	have	MAIN VERB

They *talked* on the phone.	*talked*	MAIN VERB

Did they *talk* on the phone?	*did*	AUXILIARY VERB
	talk	MAIN VERB

In French: There are only two auxiliary verbs: **avoir** (*to have*) and **être** (*to be*). The other English auxiliary verbs such as *do, does, did, will* or *would* do not exist as separate words. In French their meaning is conveyed either by a different structure (see **What are Declarative and Interrogative Sentences?**, p. 62) or by the last letters of the main verb (see **What is the Past Tense?**, p. 81, **What is the Future Tense?**, p. 91 and **What is the Conditional?**, p. 97). You will find more on this subject under the different tenses.

The verbs **avoir** and **être** are irregular verbs whose conjugations must be memorized. They are important verbs because they serve both as auxiliary verbs and main verbs.

A. *AVOIR* AND *ÊTRE* AS AUXILIARY VERBS

Every French verb is conjugated in certain tenses with either **avoir** or **être** as an auxiliary verb. Since most verbs take **avoir,** it will be easier for you to memorize only the verbs conjugated with **être.** You can assume that all the other verbs are conjugated with **avoir.** There are approximately sixteen basic verbs, sometimes referred to by grammar books as "verbs of motion," that are conjugated with **être.**

"Verbs of motion" is not an accurate description of these verbs since some of them, such as **rester** (*to stay, to remain*), do not imply motion. You will find the "**être** verbs" easier to memorize in pairs of opposites:

aller	*to go*	venir	*to come*
		retourner	*to return*
entrer	*to come in*	sortir	*to go out*
arriver	*to arrive*	partir	*to leave*
monter	*to climb*	descendre	*to go down*
rester	*to remain*	tomber	*to fall*
naître	*to be born*	mourir	*to die*

Verbs derived from the above verbs are also conjugated with **être: rentrer, revenir,** and **devenir,** among others.

A verb tense composed of an auxiliary verb plus a main verb is called a **compound verb.** The auxiliary verbs **avoir** and **être** conjugated in the different tenses and followed by the past participle of the main verb (see **What is a Participle?,** p. 76) are used to form the various tenses of the main verb. Let us look at some examples of the compound verb tenses you will encounter in your beginning study of French. (The first sentence of each pair uses a form of **avoir,** and the second, a form of **être.**)

Present of **avoir** or **être** + past participle of main verb = **passé composé** (see **What is the Past Tense?,** p. 81)

> Le garçon **a mangé** la pomme.
> *The boy **ate** (**has eaten**) the apple.*

> La fille **est allée** au cinéma.
> *The girl **went** (**has gone**) to the movies.*

Imperfect of **avoir** or **être** + past participle of main verb = **plus-que-parfait** (see **What is the Past Perfect?**, p. 87)

Le garçon **avait mangé** la pomme.
*The boy **had eaten** the apple.*

La fille **était allée** au cinéma.
*The girl **had gone** to the movies.*

Future of **avoir** or **être** + past participle of main verb = **futur antérieur** (see **What is the Future Perfect?**, p. 94)

Le garçon **aura mangé** la pomme.
*The boy **will have eaten** the apple.*

La fille **sera allée** au cinéma.
*The girl **will have gone** to the movies.*

Conditional of **avoir** or **être** + past participle of main verb = **conditionnel passé** (see **What is the Conditional?**, p. 97)

Le garçon **aurait mangé** la pomme.
*The boy **would have eaten** the apple.*

La fille **serait allée** au cinéma.
*The girl **would have gone** to the movies.*

You will learn other compound tenses as your study of French progresses.

B. *AVOIR* AND *ÊTRE* AS MAIN VERBS

The verbs **avoir** and **être** are used in the same way that you use *to have* and *to be* as main verbs in English. However, you may need a little help with two other uses of these verbs.

1. The verb **avoir** is often used in idiomatic expressions (see p. 2) where the equivalent English expression uses the verb *to be*. These expressions, like all idiomatic expressions, have to be memorized. Here are a few examples:

I *am* thirsty.   I *am* twenty years old.
   | |
  to be   to be

J'**ai** soif.   J'**ai** vingt ans.
  | |
 to have   to have

2. The English expressions *there is* and *there are* can be translated in two different ways (**il y a** or **voilà**), depending on the specific meaning you have in mind. As you study the examples below, note that **il y a** and **voilà** can be used with both one, and more than one, person or thing without changing their form; they are thus said to be **invariable.**

- **il y a**—to describe or give the location of something or someone

  Il y a un livre sur la table.
  There is a book on the table.

  Il y a beaucoup d'étudiants dans ce cours.
  There are many students in this course.

You must learn how to use this very common expression and not to use the 3rd person of **être** (**est** - *is* or **sont** - *are*) when you shouldn't.

To avoid using the wrong form, see if you can replace the *is* or *are* of the English sentence with *there is* or *there are*. If you can, you must use **il y a;** if you can't, use **est** or **sont,** whichever is correct for that sentence.

On the table *is* a book.
|
il y a

You can say: On the table *there is* a book.

The book *is* on the table.
|
est

You can't say: The book *there is* on the table.

In the room *are* chairs.
|
il y a

You can say: In the room *there are* chairs.

The chairs and tables *are* in the room.
|
sont

You can't say: The chairs and tables *there are* in the room.

- **voilà**—to point out something or someone

Voilà le livre.
There is the book.

Voilà les étudiants.
There are the students.

Notice that there is no need for a verb following **voilà.**

Practice

I. Cross out the English auxiliary verbs which are not used as auxiliaries in French?

1. Did the children do their homework?

2. They will do their homework tomorrow.

3. Do you want to do your homework now?

4. Have the children done their homework?

II. Put a checkmark under the appropriate auxiliary verb for each verb.

	AUXILIARY *ÊTRE*	AUXILIARY *AVOIR*
aller	_____	_____
avoir	_____	_____
être	_____	_____
revenir	_____	_____
manger	_____	_____
acheter	_____	_____
tomber	_____	_____

III. In the following sentences the word or words in italics correspond to one of the following French word or expressions: a) **il y a** b) **voilà** c) **est** d) **sont**

- Write your selection in the space provided.

1. Where are the students? They *are* here.   _____

2. Where is Paul? *There is* Paul, next to Mary.   _____

3. Where is Paul? He *is* next to Mary.   _____

4. In the suitcase *are* clothes and books.   _____

5. On the shelf *is* a vase.   _____

What is a Subject?

In a sentence the person or thing that performs the action is called the **subject.**[1] When you wish to find the subject of a sentence, always look for the verb first; then ask, *who?* or *what?* before the verb. The answer will be the subject.

> Paul speaks French.
>
>> *Who* speaks French?
>> Answer: Paul.
>> *Paul* is the subject.
>> (Note that the subject is singular. It refers to one person.)
>
> Are the keys on the table?
>
>> *What* is on the table?
>> Answer: the keys.
>> *Keys* is the subject.
>> (Note that the subject is plural. It refers to more than one thing.)

Train yourself to ask that question to find the subject. Never assume a word is the subject because it comes first in the sentence. Subjects can be located in several different places, as you can see in the following examples (the *subject* is in boldface and the *verb* italicized):

> *Did the game start* on time?
> After playing for two hours, *Paul became* exhausted.
> Looking in the mirror *was* a little *girl*.

Some sentences have more than one main verb; you have to find the subject of each verb.

---

[1]The subject performs the action in an active sentence, but is acted upon in a passive sentence (see **What is Meant by Active and Passive Voice?**, p. 107).

The **boys** *were doing* the cooking, while **Mary** *was setting* the table.

> *Boys* is the subject of *were doing*.
> (Note that the subject and verb are plural.)
>
> *Mary* is the subject of *was setting*.
> (Note that the subject and verb are singular.)

In both English and French it is important to find the subject of each verb to make sure that the subject and the verb agree; that is, you must choose the form of the verb that goes with the subject. (See **What is a Verb Conjugation?**, p. 51.)

Practice

Find the subjects in the following sentences.
- Next to Q, write the question you need to ask to find the subject.
- Next to A, write the answer to the question you just asked.

1. When the bell rang, all the children ran out.

    Q: _____

    A: _____

    Q: _____

    A: _____

2. One waiter took the order, another brought the food.

    Q: _____

    A: _____

    Q: _____

    A: _____

3. The first-year students voted for the class president.

    Q: _____

    A: _____

4. That assumes I am always right.

    Q: _____

    A: _____

    Q: _____

    A: _____

5. Difficult as it is, French is a beautiful language.

    Q: _____

    A: _____

    Q: _____

    A: _____

What is a Pronoun?

A **pronoun** is a word used in place of one or more nouns. It may stand, therefore, for a person, animal, place, thing, event, or idea.

For instance, rather than repeating the proper noun "Paul" in the following two sentences, it is better to use a pronoun in the second sentence.

> *Paul* likes to swim. *Paul* practices every day.
> *Paul* likes to swim. *He* practices every day.

Generally a pronoun can only be used to refer to someone (or something) that has already been mentioned. The word that the pronoun replaces or refers to is called the **antecedent** of the pronoun. In the example above, the pronoun *he* refers to the proper noun *Paul*. *Paul* is the antecedent of the pronoun *he*.

In English: There are different types of pronouns, each serving a different function and following different rules. Listed below are the more important types and the sections where they are discussed in detail.

Personal pronouns—These pronouns change their form according to the function they have in the sentence.

- as subject (see p. 45)

    I go; *they* read; *he* runs; *she* sings.

- as direct object (see p. 156)

    Paul loves *it*. Jane met *him*.

- as indirect object (see p. 156)

    Jane gave *us* the book. Speak to *them*.

- as object of a preposition (see p. 162)

    Paul is going out with *her*.

- as a disjunctive (see p. 166)

    Who is there? *Me*. Go without *her*.

Reflexive pronouns—These pronouns refer back to the subject of the sentence (see p.104).

    I cut *myself*. We washed *ourselves*.

Interrogative pronouns—These pronouns are used in questions (see p. 171).

> *Who* is that? *What* do you want?

Demonstrative pronouns—These pronouns are used to point out persons or things (see p. 182).

> *This* (one) is expensive. *That* (one) is cheap.

Possessive pronouns—These pronouns are used to show possession (see p. 189).

> Whose book is that? *Mine. Yours* is on the table.

Relative pronouns—These pronouns are used to introduce relative subordinate clauses (see p. 196).

> The man *who* came is very nice.
> That is the book *which* you read last summer.

Indefinite pronouns—These pronouns are used to refer to unidentified persons or things.

> *One* doesn't do that. *Something* is wrong.

Since the indefinite pronouns in French correspond in usage to their English equivalents, there is no special section devoted to this type of pronoun. The various indefinite pronouns can be studied in your textbook and memorized as vocabulary.

In French: Pronouns are identified in the same way as in English. The most important difference is that a pronoun agrees with the noun it replaces; that is, it must correspond in gender, and usually in number, with its antecedent.

Practice

The following sentences contain different types of pronouns.
- Circle the pronouns.
- Draw an arrow from the pronoun to its antecedent, or antecedents if there is more than one.

1. Did Mary call Peter? Yes, she called him last night.

2. The coat and dress are elegant, but they are expensive.

3. Mary baked the cookies herself.

4. Paul and I are very tired. We went out last night.

5. If the book is not on the bed, look under it.

What is a Subject Pronoun?

A **subject pronoun** is a pronoun used as a subject of a verb.

> *He* worked while *she* read.

>> Who worked? Answer: He.
>> *He* is the subject of the verb *worked*.

>> Who read? Answer: She.
>> *She* is the subject of the verb *read*.

Subject pronouns are divided into the following categories: the person speaking (the **first person**), the person spoken to (the **second person**), and the person spoken about (the **third person**). These categories are further divided into singular and plural.

Let us compare the personal subject pronouns in English and French.

	ENGLISH	FRENCH
SINGULAR		
1st PERSON	*I*	**je**
the person speaking		
2nd PERSON	*you*	**tu**
the person spoken to		
3rd PERSON	*he*	**il**
the person or object spoken about	*she*	**elle**
	it	
PLURAL		
1st PERSON	*we*	**nous**
the person speaking plus others		

    Paul and *I* speak French.
        we

2nd PERSON	*you*	**vous**
the persons spoken to		

    Paul and *you* like to speak French.
        you

3rd PERSON	*they*	**ils**
the persons or objects spoken about		**elles**

    Paul and *Mary* speak French.
        they

There are three English subject pronouns which have more than one equivalent in French: *you, it* and *they*. Let us look at each one so that you can learn how to choose the correct form.

YOU - **tu** or **vous**

In English: *You* is always used to address the person or persons you are talking to. The same pronoun *you* is used to address the President of the United States or your dog.

> Do *you* have any questions, Mr. President.
> *You* are a good dog, Snoopy.

Also, there is no difference between *you* in the singular and *you* in the plural. For example, if there were many people standing in a room and you asked: "Are *you* coming with me?" the *you* could refer to one person or to more than one.

In French: There are two sets of pronouns for *you:*

1. The **familiar form**—**tu** singular (**vous** plural) This form is used when you speak to a child, family member, a friend, an animal, or anyone with whom you are not on formal terms.

2. The **formal form**—**vous** singular (**vous** plural) This form, also called the **polite form,** is used to address one or more persons you do not know very well.

Note: When in doubt, always use the polite form, unless speaking to a child or animal, because you are likely to offend French speakers by addressing them with **tu** when it is not appropriate.

See pp. 52–54 for a more detailed study of these forms.

IT - **il** or **elle**

In English: Whenever you refer to one thing or idea, you use the pronoun *it.*

> Where is the book? *It* is on the table.
> Paul had a good idea. *It* is interesting.

In French: The singular pronoun you use depends on the gender of the noun it replaces (see **What is Meant by Gender?**, p. 7); that is, the pronoun must correspond in gender with its antecedent. If the antecedent is masculine, use the pronoun **il.** If the antecedent is feminine, use the pronoun **elle.**

> Où est le livre? **Il** est sur la table.
> | |
>   masc. sing. masc. sing.
>   antecedent   pronoun

Where is the book? It is on the table.

> Paul a eu une bonne idée. **Elle** est intéressante.
> | |
>   fem. sing. fem. sing.
>   antecedent pronoun

Paul had a good idea. It is interesting.

THEY - **ils** or **elles**

In English: Whenever you refer to more than one person or more than one object you use the plural pronoun *they.*

> My brothers like sports; *they* play tennis.
> Where are the books? *They* are on the table.
> I can't buy flowers; *they* cost too much.

In French: The plural pronoun you use depends on the gender of the noun it replaces, that is, of the antecedent.

If the antecedent is masculine, use the pronoun **ils.**

> Mes frères aiment les sports; **ils** jouent au tennis.
> | |
>   masc. pl.   masc. pl.
>   antecedent   pronoun

My brothers like sports. They play tennis.

Où sont les livres? **Ils** sont sur la table.
                 | |
              masc. pl. masc. pl.
              antecedent pronoun

*Where are the books? **They** are on the table.*

If the antecedent is feminine, use the pronoun **elles.**

Je ne peux pas acheter de fleurs; **elles** coûtent trop cher.
                          | |
                      fem. pl. fem. pl.
                 antecedent pronoun

*I can't buy flowers; **they** cost too much.*

If there is more than one antecedent of the same gender, the pronoun will be **ils** if both antecedents are masculine, or **elles** if both antecedents are feminine.

J'aime cette robe et cette blouse. **Elles** sont jolies.
           | | |
         fem. sing.   fem. sing. fem. pl.
           └ antecedents ┘   pronoun

*I like this dress and this blouse. **They** are pretty.*

If there is more than one antecedent of different genders, the pronoun will always be **ils.**

J'aime cette robe et ce manteau. **Ils** sont élégants.
           | | |
         fem. sing.   masc. sing. masc. pl.
         └ antecedents ┘   pronoun

*I like this dress and this coat. **They** are elegant.*

Practice

I. In the space provided, fill in the English and French subject pronouns which correspond to the PERSON and NUMBER indicated.

PERSON	NUMBER	SUBJECT	
		ENGLISH	FRENCH
1. 1st	sing.	_____	_____
2. 3rd	pl.	_____	_____
3. 2nd	sing.	_____	_____
4. 1st	pl.	_____	_____
5. 2nd	pl.	_____	_____
6. 3rd	sing.	_____	_____

II. Write the French subject pronoun that you would use to replace the words in italics:

	FRENCH SUBJECT PRONOUN
1. *I* am very tired.	_____
2. Come on children, *you* must go to bed now.	_____
3. *Paul and I* are going out.	_____
4. Mommy, *you* have to give me a kiss.	_____
5. *Mary and Helen* are home.	_____
6. Professor Morton, *you* haven't given us our homework.	_____
7. Do *you and your wife* like sports?	_____
8. *My brother and sister* speak French.	_____

What is a Verb Conjugation?

A **verb conjugation** is a list of the six possible forms of the verb for a particular tense. For each tense, there is one verb form for each of the six persons used as the subject of the verb. (See **What is a Subject Pronoun?**, p. 45.)

In English: Most verbs change very little. Let us look at the various forms of the verb *to sing* when each of the possible pronouns is the subject.[1]

> SINGULAR
>   1st PERSON   I *sing* with the music.
>   2nd PERSON   You *sing* with the music.
>
>   He *sings* with the music.
>   3rd PERSON   She *sings* with the music.
>   It *sings* with the music.
>
> PLURAL
>   1st PERSON   We *sing* with the music.
>   2nd PERSON   You *sing* with the music.
>   3rd PERSON   They *sing* with the music.

Because English verbs change so little, you do not need to "conjugate verbs." It is much simpler to say that verbs add an "-s" in the 3rd person singular.

In French: Verb forms change constantly, and it is therefore necessary to know the form of the verb for each of the six persons for each tense. Memorizing all the forms of all the verbs that exist would be an impossible, endless task. Fortunately, most French verbs belong to the first of the following two categories:

Regular verbs–Verbs whose forms follow a regular pattern; only one example must be memorized and the pattern can then be applied to other verbs in the same group.

---

[1]In this section we will talk about the present tense only (see **What is the Present Tense?**, p. 71).

Irregular verbs—Verbs whose forms do not follow any regular pattern and must be memorized individually.

A. SUBJECT

Let us now conjugate in French the verb **chanter** (*to sing*). Pay special attention to the subject.

SINGULAR	
1st PERSON	**je** chante
2nd PERSON	**tu** chantes
3rd PERSON	**il** chante
	elle chante

PLURAL	
1st PERSON	**nous** chantons
2nd PERSON	**vous** chantez
3rd PERSON	**ils** chantent
	elles chantent

Each subject represents the doer of the action of the verb.

1st person singular—The *I form* of the verb (the **je** form) is used whenever the person speaking is the doer of the action.

Le matin **je chante** bien.
*In the morning **I sing** well.*

2nd person singular—The *you familiar singular form* of the verb (the **tu** form) is used whenever the person spoken to (with whom you are on familiar terms, see p. 47) is the doer of the action.

Jean, **tu chantes** bien.
*John, **you sing** well.*

3rd person singular—The *he, she, it form* of the verb (the **il, elle** form) is used when the person, thing, or idea spoken about is the doer of the action. The 3rd person singular subject can be expressed in one of three ways:

1. by the third person singular masculine pronoun **il** (*he*, *it*) and the third person singular feminine pronoun **elle** (*she*, *it*)

Il chante bien.   Regardez ce livre. **Il** est intéressant.
He sings well.   *Look at this book. It is interesting.*

Elle chante bien.   Voici la voiture. **Elle** est chère.
She sings well.   *Here is the car. It is expensive.*

2. by one proper name

Marie **chante** bien.
Mary sings well.

3. by a singular noun

Le garçon **chante** bien.
The boy sings well.

L'oiseau **chante** bien.
The bird sings well.

1st person plural–The *we form* of the verb (the **nous** form) is used whenever "I" (the speaker) is one of the doers of the action; that is, whenever the speaker is included in a plural or multiple subject.

Marie, Paul et moi **chantons** bien.
Mary, Paul and I sing well.

> In this sentence, the subject, *Mary, Paul and I,* could be replaced by the pronoun *we,* so that in French you must use the **nous** form of the verb.

2nd person plural–The *you plural polite form* of the verb (the **vous** form) is used in two instances:

1. when two or more persons with whom you use **tu** individually are the doers of the action.

>   Paul et Marie, vous **chantez** bien.
>   Paul, **tu chantes** bien.
>   Marie, **tu chantes** bien.
>   *Paul and Mary, you sing well.*

2. when one or more persons whom you address formally are the doers of the action.

>   Madame Dupont, vous **chantez** bien.
>   *Mrs. Dupont, you sing well.*

>   Monsieur et Madame Dupont, vous **chantez** bien.
>   *Mr. and Mrs. Dupont, you sing well.*

3rd person plural—The *they form* of the verb (the **ils, elles** form) is used when the persons, things, or ideas which are spoken about are the doers of the action. The 3rd person plural subject can be expressed in one of three ways:

1. by the third person plural masculine pronoun **ils** (*they*) and the third person plural feminine pronoun **elles** (*they*)

>   **Ils chantent** bien.   Lis ces livres. **Ils** sont faciles.
>   *They sing well.*   *Read these books. They are easy.*

>   **Elles chantent** bien.   Achète ces robes. **Elles** sont jolies.
>   *They sing well.*   *Buy these dresses. They are pretty.*

2. by two or more proper or common nouns

>   Marie et Paul **chantent** bien.
>   *Mary and Paul sing well.*

>   La fille et son père **chantent** bien.
>   *The girl and her father sing well.*

3. by a plural noun

    Les filles **chantent** bien.
    *The girls **sing** well.*

B. VERB FORM

Let us again look at the conjugation of the same verb *to sing,* paying special attention to the verb forms. Notice that each of the six persons has a different verb form. However, when two pronouns belong to the same person there is only one verb form. For instance, the 3rd person singular has two pronouns, **il** and **elle,** but they both have the same verb form: **chante.**

je	chante
tu	chant**es**
il	chante
elle	
nous	chant**ons**
vous	chant**ez**
ils	chant**ent**
elles	

The French verb is composed of two parts:

1. The **stem** (also called the **root**), **la racine** in French, which is found by dropping the last two or three letters from the infinitive (see **What is the Infinitive?,** p. 30).

INFINITIVE	STEM
chant**er**	chant-
fin**ir**	fin-
vend**re**	vend-

In regular verbs the stem rarely changes throughout a conjugation.

2. The **ending, la terminaison** in French, which changes for each person in the conjugation of regular and irregular verbs. You will know which endings to add when you have established which group the verb belongs to.

VERB GROUPS

Regular verbs are divided into three groups, also called **conjugations,** based on the infinitive ending.

-er	-ir	-re
1st GROUP	2nd GROUP	3rd GROUP

Each of the three verb groups has its own set of verb endings for each tense (see **What is Meant by Tense?,** p 69). You will have to memorize all the tenses of only one sample verb from each group in order to conjugate any regular verb belonging to that group. As an example, let us look more closely at regular verbs of the first group, that is, verbs like **parler** (*to speak*) and **aimer** (*to love*) that follow the pattern of **chanter** (*to sing*), conjugated above.

1. Identify the group of the verb by its infinitive ending.

> parl**er**   1st conjugation or group
> aim**er**

2. Find the verb stem by removing the infinitive ending.

> parl-
> aim-

3. Add the ending that agrees with the subject.

> je parle   j'aime
> tu parle**s**   tu aime**s**
>
> il parle   il aime
> elle parle   elle aime

nous parl**ons**	nous aim**ons**
vous parl**ez**	vous aim**ez**
ils parl**ent**	ils aim**ent**
elles parl**ent**	elles aim**ent**

The endings for verbs belonging to the other groups will be different, but the process of conjugation will always be the same for regular verbs:

1. Identify the group of the verb by its infinitive ending.
2. Find the verb stem.
3. According to the group, add the ending that agrees with the subject.

A special word must be said about the verbs of the first group. Although you can easily see the differences among the various verb forms when they are written (*chante, chantes, chantent*), they are all pronounced in the same way (*chante*). In order to write them correctly you will have to identify the subject.

As irregular verbs are introduced in your textbook, the entire conjugation will be given so that you can memorize them individually. Be sure to do so because many common verbs are irregular (**avoir,** *to have,* **être,** *to be,* and **faire,** *to make,* for example).

Practice

I. This is the regular verb **finir** (*to finish*) conjugated in the present tense:

je finis	nous finissons
tu finis	vous finissez
il/elle finit	ils/elles finissent

- Circle the stem of the verb above.
- Box in the ending of each person of the verb above.

- Now, conjugate the regular verb **choisir** (*to choose*) by filling in the spaces below.

je _____   nous _____

tu _____   vous _____

il/elle _____   ils/elles _____

II. This is the regular verb **répondre** (*to answer*) conjugated in the present tense:

je réponds   nous répondons

tu réponds   vous répondez

il/elle répond   ils/elles répondent

- Circle the stem of the verb above.
- Box in the ending of each person of the verb above.
- Now, conjugate the regular verb **vendre** (*to sell*) by filling in the spaces below.

je _____   nous _____

tu _____   vous _____

il/elle _____   ils/elles _____

What are Affirmative and Negative Sentences?

A sentence can be classified as to whether it is expressing a fact or situation that is or a fact or situation that is not.

An **affirmative sentence** expresses a fact or situation that is; it *affirms* the information.

> France is a country in Europe.
> Paul will work at the university.
> They liked to travel.

A **negative sentence** expresses a fact or situation that is not; it *negates* the information. It includes a word of negation.

> France is *not* a country in Asia.
> Paul will *not* work at the university.
> They did *not* like to travel.

In English: An affirmative sentence can become a negative sentence in one of two ways:

- by adding the word **not** after some verbs

AFFIRMATIVE	NEGATIVE
Paul is a student.	Paul is *not* a student.
Mary can do it.	Mary *cannot* do it.
They will travel.	They will *not* travel.

Frequently, the word *not* is attached to the verb and the letter "o" is replaced by an apostrophe; this is called a **contraction.** The contracted form of "will not" is "won't."

> Paul *isn't* a student.
> |
>   is not

> Mary *can't* do it.
> |
>   cannot

> They *won't* travel.
> |
>   will not

- by adding the auxiliary verb *do, does,* or *did* + *not* + the dictionary form of the main verb (*do* or *does* is used for negatives in the
present tense and *did* for negatives in the past tense—see **What is
the Present Tense?**, p. 71 and **What is the Past Tense?**, p. 81)

AFFIRMATIVE	NEGATIVE
We study a lot.	We *do not study* a lot.
Mary writes well.	Mary *does not write* well.
The train arrived.	The train *did not arrive.*

Frequently, *do, does,* or *did* is contracted with *not: don't, doesn't,
didn't.*

In French: The basic rule for turning an affirmative sentence into a
negative sentence is to put **ne** before the conjugated verb and **pas**
after that verb.

AFFIRMATIVE	NEGATIVE
Nous étudions beaucoup.	Nous **n'**étudions **pas** beaucoup.
	conjugated verb
We study a lot.	*We **do not** study a lot.*
Marie écrit bien.	Marie **n'**écrit **pas** bien.
	conjugated verb
Mary writes well.	*Mary **does not** write well.*
Le train est arrivé.	Le train **n'**est **pas** arrivé.
	conjugated verb
The train arrived.	*The train **did not** arrive.*

The placement of **ne** and **pas** varies somewhat when an infinitive is
negated and when there is an object pronoun in the sentence. Be sure
to consult your textbook.

Remember that there is no equivalent for the auxiliary words *do, does, did* in French; do not try to include them in a negative sentence.

Practice

I. The following are affirmative sentences.
 • Write the negative of each sentence on the line below.

1. We want to speak English in class.

_____

2. He did his homework yesterday.

_____

3. Helen was home yesterday.

_____

4. Paul can go to the restaurant with us.

_____

5. Paul and Mary drove to Paris.

_____

II. Go over the sentences you have just written.
 • Circle the elements which indicate the negative.

III. Box in the English words around which you would place the **ne . . . pas** in a French sentence.

What are Declarative and Interrogative Sentences?

A sentence can be classified according to its purpose.

A **declarative sentence** is a sentence that is a statement; it *declares* the information.

> Columbus discovered America in 1492.

An **interrogative sentence** is a sentence that asks a question.

> When did Columbus discover America?

In written language, an interrogative sentence always ends with a question mark.

In English: A declarative sentence can be changed to an interrogative sentence in one of two ways:

1. by adding the auxiliary verb *do, does,* or *did* before the subject and changing the main verb to the dictionary form of the verb (*do* and *does* are used to introduce a question in the present tense and *did* to introduce a question in the past tense—see **What is the Present Tense?**, p. 71 and **What is the Past Tense?**, p. 81)

DECLARATIVE	→	INTERROGATIVE
Philip *likes* intelligent girls.		*Does* Philip *like* intelligent girls?
Paul and Mary *sing* together.		*Do* Paul and Mary *sing* together?
Alice *went* to Paris.		*Did* Alice *go* to Paris?

2. by using an **inversion** of some verbs, that is inverting the normal word order of subject + verb to verb + subject

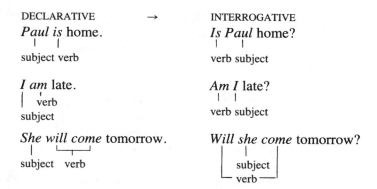

In French: A declarative sentence can be changed to an interrogative sentence in one of two ways:

1. by adding the expression **est-ce que** before the statement

> Philippe aime la France.
> **Est-ce que** Philippe aime la France?
> *Philip likes France.*
> **Does** *Philip like France?*

> Paul et Marie chantent ensemble.
> **Est-ce que** Paul et Marie chantent ensemble?
> *Paul and Mary sing together.*
> **Do** *Paul and Mary sing together?*

> Paul est à la maison.
> **Est-ce que** Paul est à la maison?
> *Paul is home.*
> **Is Paul** *home?*

Make sure that you ignore *do, does* and *did* when you are using French. Just like **est-ce que,** they signal a question, but they are not translated.

2. by using inversion, that is, by putting the subject after the verb

If the subject is a pronoun, simply invert the verb and pronoun subject.

> Vous êtes à la maison ce soir.
> **Etes-vous** à la maison ce soir?
> *You are home this evening.*
> *Are you home this evening?*

If the subject is a noun, follow these steps:

1. State the noun subject.
2. State the verb and, when writing, add a hyphen.
3. State the subject pronoun that corresponds to the gender and number of the subject (see p. 52).

> Paul est à la maison ce soir.
> **Paul** est-**il** à la maison ce soir?

```
        |     |
        |  verb|
noun          pronoun subject
subject
```

> *Paul is home this evening.*
> *Is Paul home this evening?*
> (Word-for-word: ***Paul*** is ***he*** home this evening?)

> La montre et la clé sont sur la table.
> **La montre et la clé** sont-**elles** sur la table?

> Since both subjects (*la montre* and *la clé*) are feminine, the pronoun will be feminine plural; i.e., *elles*.

> *The watch and the key are on the table.*
> *Are the watch and the key on the table?*
> (Word-for-word: ***The watch and the key*** are ***they*** on the table?)

Paul et Hélène chantent ensemble.
Paul et Hélène chantent-**ils** ensemble?

> Since one subject is masculine (*Paul*) and the other feminine
> (*Hélène*), the pronoun will be masculine plural; i.e., *ils*. (See
> p. 49.)

Paul and Helen sing together.
Do Paul and Helen sing together?

Note: These are the two basic forms for asking a question. Be sure
to use only one form or the other, either **est-ce que** with no inversion
of the verb and subject or the inversion form.

TAG QUESTIONS

In both English and French when you expect a yes-or-no answer, you can
also transform a statement into a question by adding a short phrase at the
end of the statement. This short phrase is sometimes called a **tag.**

In English: The tag repeats the idea of the statement as a negative
question.

Paul and Mary sing together, *don't they?*
Philip likes France, *doesn't he?*
The watch and the key are on the table, *aren't they?*

In French: The words **n'est-ce pas?** can be added to a declarative
sentence to turn it into a question.

Paul et Mary chantent ensemble, **n'est-ce pas?**
*Paul and Mary sing together, **don't they?***

Philippe aime la France, **n'est-ce pas?**
*Philip likes France, **doesn't he?***

La montre et la clé sont sur la table, **n'est-ce pas?**
*The watch and the key are on the table, **aren't they?***

Notice that although the expression **n'est-ce pas** never changes, the
English equivalent does.

Practice

I. The following are declarative sentences.
- Write the interrogative of each sentence on the line below.

1. Paul and Mary studied all evening.

_____

2. His brother eats a lot.

_____

3. The girl's parents speak French.

_____

II. Look at the sentences you have just written.
- Circle the words which indicate the interrogative.

III. The following is a declarative sentence.

My mother and father went to the movies.

Let us see the different ways it can be changed to an interrogative sentence in French.

- In the sentence above, box in the word before which you would place **est-ce que?**
- Circle the word after which you would place **n'est-ce pas?**
- In the blanks below, fill in the 3 steps you would follow to use the inversion form.
- Fill in the answers to the 3 steps.
- In the space provided, fill in the answer to step 3 in French.

1. State the _____ : _____

2. State the _____ : _____

3. State the _____ that corresponds to the subject:

_____ In French : _____

What is Meant by Mood?

Verb forms are divided into "moods" which, in turn, are subdivided into one or more tenses. The word *mood* is a variation of the word *mode,* meaning manner or way. The various moods indicate the attitude of the speaker toward what he or she is saying. For instance, if you are making a statement you use one mood, but if you are giving an order you use another. As a beginning student of French, you only have to recognize the names of the moods so that you will know what your French textbook is referring to when it uses these terms. You will learn when to use the various moods as you learn verbs and their tenses.

In English: Verbs can be in one of three moods:

1. The **indicative mood** is used to state the action of the verb, that is, to *indicate* facts. This is the most common mood, and most of the verb forms that you use in everyday conversation belong to the indicative mood. The tenses studied in this handbook belong to the indicative mood: the present tense (see p. 71), the past tense (see p. 81), and the future tense (p. 91) are all examples of tenses in the indicative mood.

    Paul *studies* French.
    present indicative

    Mary *was* here.
    past indicative

    They *will come* tomorrow.
    future indicative

2. The **imperative mood** is used to express the action of the verb in the form of a command (see **What is the Imperative?**, p. 73). This mood is not divided into tenses.

    Paul, *study* French now!
    Mary, *be* home on time!

3. The **subjunctive mood** is used to express an attitude or feeling toward the action of the verb. Since it stresses feelings about the fact or idea, it is "subjective" about them. (See **What is the Subjunctive?**, p. 114.) This mood is not divided into tenses.

> The school requires that students *study* French.
> I wish that Mary *were* here.
> The teacher recommends that he *do* his homework.

In French: The French language identifies four moods.

1. As in English, the indicative mood is the most common, and most of the tenses you will learn belong to this mood.

2. The imperative mood is also used to give orders.

3. The subjunctive mood is used much more frequently than in English. The French subjunctive has two tenses: the present subjunctive and the past subjunctive. The present subjunctive is commonly used in conversation and in written French. Textbooks use the term "present subjunctive" to distinguish that tense from the "present indicative" and the "present conditional." Modern French usage has all but discarded the past subjunctive. Nowadays, it is never used in conversation and only occasionally in writing.

4. The **conditional mood** (see p. 97) is used to express the action of the verb as a possibility or an impossibility. There are two tenses: the present conditional and the past conditional.

> Si j'avais de l'argent, j'**achèterais** ce livre.
> *If I had money,* I **would buy** *this book.*

> Les étudiants **seraient allés** à Paris, s'ils avaient eu le temps.
> *The students* **would have gone** *to Paris, if they had had the time.*

Textbooks use the term "present conditional" to distinguish it from the "present indicative" and "present subjunctive." If no reference is made to the mood, it usually belongs to the most common, the indicative.

Practice

Fill in the blanks.

Mood is a term used in reference to (1) _____ , not nouns.
The most common mood in English and in French is the
(2) _____ mood. The (3) _____ ,
(4) _____ , and (5) _____ are examples of some of
the tenses in this mood. When I order someone to do something, I am
using the (6) _____ mood. The third mood is the
(7) _____ which is used to stress the speaker's attitude
toward what he or she is saying. French also has another mood called the
(8) _____ .

What is Meant by Tense?

The **tense** of a verb indicates the time when the action of the verb takes
place (at the present time, in the past, or in the future). The word *tense*
comes from the same word as the French word "temps," which means
time.

I am eating.	PRESENT
I ate.	PAST
I will eat.	FUTURE

As you can see in the above examples, just by putting the verb in a
different tense and without giving any additional information (such as "I
am eating *now*," "I ate *yesterday*," "I will eat *tomorrow*,"), you can
indicate when the action of the verb takes place.

Tenses may be classified according to the way they are formed. A **simple tense** consists of only one verb form, while a **compound tense** consists of two or more verb forms.

In English: There are only two simple tenses: the present and the past.

I study	PRESENT
I studied	PAST

All of the other tenses are compound tenses formed by one or more auxiliary verbs plus the main verb.

I have studied	PRESENT PERFECT
I was studying	PAST PROGRESSIVE
I will study	FUTURE
I will have studied	FUTURE PERFECT
I would study	CONDITIONAL[1]
I would have studied	PAST CONDITIONAL

In French: There are more simple tenses than in English.

j'étudie	PRESENT
j'étudiai	SIMPLE PAST
j'étudiais	IMPERFECT
j'étudierai	FUTURE
j'étudierais	CONDITIONAL[1]

There are also compound tenses in French. They are formed by the auxiliary verbs **avoir** or **être** + the past participle of the main verb.

j'ai étudié	*I have studied*	PRESENT PERFECT
j'avais étudié	*I had studied*	PAST PERFECT
j'aurai étudié	*I will have studied*	FUTURE PERFECT
j'aurais étudié	*I would have studied*	PAST CONDITIONAL

---

[1]We have included the conditional because it is conjugated like a verb tense, but we have omitted the subjunctive because it has no parallel in English.

This handbook discusses these tenses in separate sections: **What is the Past Tense?**, p. 81; **What is the Past Perfect?**, p. 87; **What is the Future Perfect?**, p. 94, and **What is the Conditional?**, p. 97.

Practice

Fill in the blanks.

The word tense refers to the (1) _____ an action takes place. A (2) _____ tense consists of one verb form; a compound tense consists of (3) _____ or more verb forms: the (4) _____ verb (or verbs) plus the (5) _____ verb. The (6) _____ and the (7) _____ tenses are examples of two simple tenses in English. French has more (8) _____ tenses than English. For instance the (9) _____ is a (10) _____ tense in French and a compound tense in English.

What is the Present Tense?

The **present tense** indicates that the action is happening at the present time. It can be:

when the speaker is speaking	I *see* you.
a habitual action	He *smokes* when he *is* nervous.
a general truth	The sun *shines* every day.

In English: There are three forms of the verb which indicate the present tense, although they have slightly different meanings:

Mary *studies* in the library.   PRESENT
Mary *is studying* in the library.   PRESENT PROGRESSIVE
Mary *does study* in the library.   PRESENT EMPHATIC

When you answer the following questions, you will automatically choose one of the above forms.

Where does Mary study?
Mary *studies* in the library.

Where is Mary now?
Mary *is studying* in the library.

Does Mary study in the library?
Yes, Mary *does study* in the library.

In French: There is only one verb form to indicate the present tense. It is used to express the meaning of the English present, present progressive, and present emphatic tenses. In French the idea of the present tense is indicated by the ending of the verb, without any auxiliary verb such as *is* and *does*. It is very important, therefore, not to translate these English auxiliary verbs. Simply put the main verb in the present tense.

*Mary **studies** in the library.*
étudie

*Mary **is studying** in the library.*
étudie

*Mary **does study** in the library.*
étudie

Practice

I. The following are sentences in the present tense.
- Fill in the proper form of the verb *to read* in the following answers.

1. What does Mary do all day?

    She _____ .

2. Has she read *The Red and the Black*?

    No, but she _____ it right now.

3. Does Mary read French?

    Yes, she _____ French.

II. In French, the answer to question 1 above is the verb form **lit,** from the verb **lire** (*to read*).
- In the spaces provided, write the French verb form for the answers to questions 2 and 3.

   2. _____   3. _____

What is the Imperative?

The **imperative** is the command form of a verb. It is used to give someone an order. There are affirmative commands (an order to do something) and negative commands (an order not to do something).

In English: There are two types of commands.

1. The **you** *command* is used when giving an order to one person or many persons. The dictionary form of the verb is used for the *you* command.

AFFIRMATIVE	NEGATIVE
Answer the phone.	Don't *answer* the phone.
Clean your room.	Don't *clean* your room.
Talk softly.	Don't *talk* softly.

Notice that the pronoun "you" is not stated. The absence of the pronoun *you* in the sentence is a good indication that you are dealing with an imperative and not a present tense.

2. The **we** *command* is used when the speaker gives a suggestion to himself as well as to others. In English this form begins with the phrase "let us" followed by the dictionary form of the verb.

AFFIRMATIVE	NEGATIVE
Let us leave.	*Let us not leave.*
Let us go to the movies.	*Let us not go* to the movies.

In French: There are also two basic types of commands, but there are three forms because the *you command* has both a familiar and a formal form. Most verbs are regular and use the present tense without the subject pronoun.

1. The **tu** *command*

AFFIRMATIVE	NEGATIVE
Viens ici.	**Ne viens pas** ici.
Come here.	*Don't come here.*
Chante.	**Ne chante pas.**
Sing.	*Don't sing.*

Notice that verbs of the first group (**-er** verbs) drop the final "s" of the **tu** form of the present tense (present = **tu** chantes/imperative = chante).

2. The **vous** command

AFFIRMATIVE
Venez ici.
Come here.

Chantez.
Sing.

NEGATIVE
Ne venez pas ici.
Don't come here.

Ne chantez pas.
Don't sing.

3. The **nous** command

AFFIRMATIVE
Allons.
Let us go.

Chantons.
Let us sing.

NEGATIVE
N'allons pas.
Let us not go.

Ne chantons pas.
Let us not sing.

Practice

I. Change the following sentences to the imperative affirmative.

1. You should study every evening.

_____

2. We go to the movies once a week.

_____

II. Change the following sentences to the imperative negative.

1. You shouldn't sleep in class.

_____

2. We don't speak in class.

_____

III. The following are five sentences in French.
  • Indicate if the verb of the sentences below is in the Imperative (I) or the Present (P) by circling the appropriate letter.

1. Tu lis beaucoup.   I   P

2. Parlons français.   I   P

3. Vous allez en France.   I   P

4. Etudie.   I   P

5. Ne dormons pas.   I   P

What is a Participle?

A **participle** has two functions: 1. It is a form of the verb that is used in combination with an auxiliary verb to indicate certain tenses. 2. It may be used as an adjective or modifier to describe something.

> I *was writing* a letter.
>   auxiliary participle

> The *broken* vase was on the floor.
>   participle describing *vase*

There are two types of participles: the **present participle** and the **past participle.** As you will learn, participles are not used in the same way in English and French.

A. THE PRESENT PARTICIPLE

In English: The present participle is easy to recognize because it is the *-ing* form of the verb: *working, studying, dancing, playing.*

The present participle is used:

- as an adjective

> This is an *amazing* discovery.
> describes the noun *discovery*

> He was a good *dancing* partner.
> describes the noun *partner*

- in a verbal function

1. as the main verb in compound tenses (see p. 33)

> She is *singing*.
> present progressive of *to sing*

> They were *dancing*.
> past progressive of *to dance*

2. in a participial phrase

> (By) *studying* hard, Philip learned English.
> participial phrase

> I burned myself (while) *cooking*.
> participial phrase

In French: The present participle is formed by adding **-ant** to the stem of the **nous** form of the present tense.

PRESENT	STEM	PRESENT PARTICIPLE
chantons	chant-	chant**ant**
finissons	finiss-	finiss**ant**
répondons	répond-	répond**ant**
recevons	recev-	recev**ant**

The present participle is not used the same way in French as in English, and it is usually introduced at an advanced level of French.

As a beginner, you must keep in mind that the French equivalents of the common English tenses formed with an auxiliary + present participle (*she is singing, they were dancing*) do not use participles in French. These English constructions correspond to a simple tense of a French verb.

| *She is singing.* | = | Elle **chante.** |
| present progressive | | present |

| *They were dancing.* | = | Ils **dansaient.** |
| past progressive | | imperfect |

| *He will be writing.* | = | Il **écrira.** |
| future progressive | | future |

Note: Never assume that an English word ending with *-ing* is translated by its French counterpart ending in **-ant**. The French present participle is used much less frequently than the English present participle, and as a beginning student of French you will probably not encounter it.

B. THE PAST PARTICIPLE

In English: The past participle is formed in several ways. You can always find it by remembering the form of the verb that follows *I have: I have spoken, I have written, I have walked.*

The past participle is used:

* as an adjective

> Is the *written* word more important than the *spoken* word?
> | |
> describes the noun *word*   describes the noun *word*

* as a verb form in combination with the auxiliary verb *have*

> I have *written* all that I have to say.
> He hasn't *spoken* to me since our quarrel.

In French: Regular verbs have a regular past participle:

> **-er** verbs add **-é** to the stem
> **-ir** verbs add **-i** to the stem
> **-re** verbs add **-u** to the stem

INFINITIVE	STEM	PAST PARTICIPLE
chanter	chant-	chanté
finir	fin-	fini
répondre	répond-	répondu

You will have to memorize irregular past participles individually. As you can see in the examples below, they may be very different from the infinitive.

INFINITIVE	PAST PARTICIPLE
être	été
avoir	eu
recevoir	reçu
comprendre	compris
écrire	écrit

As in English, the past participle can be used as an adjective or a verb form.

- When the past participle is used as an adjective, it must agree with the noun it modifies in gender and in number.

> *the* **spoken** language
>
>> *Spoken* modifies the noun *language*. Since **la langue** (*language*) is feminine singular, the word for *spoken* must be feminine singular. This is shown by adding an **-e.**
>
> la langue **parlée**

> *the* **written** words
>
>> *Written* modifies the noun *words*. Since **les mots** (*words*) is masculine plural, the word for *written* must be masculine plural. This is shown by adding an **-s.**
>
> les mots **écrits**

- The most important use of the past participle in French is as a verb form. Many past tenses are formed with the auxiliary verbs **avoir** and **être** and the past participle. (See **What is the Past Tense?**, p. 81.)

Practice

I. Fill in the blanks.

In English, the (1) "- _____" form of the verb as in "singing" is an example of the (2) _____ participle. The (3) _____ participle is the form of the verb following "I have." *Begun* is an example of a (4) _____ participle. In beginning French, you will rarely encounter (5) _____ participles.

II. The following are sentences in the present tense.
- Circle the auxiliary + present participles. They are the equivalent of a simple tense in French.

1. I am speaking French.
2. Paul and Mary were studying for the exam.
3. Are you bringing the book to class?
4. The students will be trying to memorize the verbs.

What is the Past Tense?

The **past tense** is used to express an action that occurred in the past.

In English: There are several verb forms that indicate the action took place in the past.

I worked	SIMPLE PAST
I was working	PAST PROGRESSIVE
I used to work	WITH HELPING VERB used to
I did work	PAST EMPHATIC
I have worked	PRESENT PERFECT
I had worked	PAST PERFECT

The simple past is called "simple" because it is a simple tense; i.e., it consists of one word (*worked* in the example above). The other past tenses are compound tenses; i.e., they consist of more than one word (*was working, did work,* etc.). The past perfect is discussed in a separate section (see p. 87).

In French: There are many verb tenses that express an action which occurred in the past. Each tense has its own set of endings and its own rules which tell us when and how to use it. We are concerned here with only two of the past tenses in French: the **passé composé** (*the present perfect*) and the **imparfait** (*the imperfect*).

A. THE PRESENT PERFECT

The **passé composé** is formed by the auxiliary verb **avoir** (*to have*) or **être** (*to be*) conjugated in the present tense + the past participle of the main verb. As in English, the past participle is not conjugated (i.e., it does not change form from one person to another: *I* have *written. He* has *written.*)

      j'ai parlé   *I spoke, I have spoken*
      je suis allé   *I went, I have gone*

There are two steps to follow in forming this tense:

1. Determine whether the verb takes **avoir** or **être** as the auxiliary (see **What are Auxiliary Verbs?**, p. 33).

2. Depending on which auxiliary verb is required, apply the following rules of agreement.

- if the auxiliary verb is **être,** the past participle agrees with the subject (review the section **What is a Subject?**, p. 40)

    Pierre est **allé** au cinéma.
     | |
    subject   past participle
      └ masc. sing. ┘

    Peter **went** *to the movies.*

    Marie est **allée** au cinéma.
     | |
    subject   past participle
      └ fem. sing. ┘

    Mary **went** *to the movies.*

Pierre et Marie sont **allés** au cinéma.

subjects   past participle
     masc. pl.

*Peter and Mary **went** to the movies.*

- if the auxiliary is **avoir,** the past participle agrees with the direct object if it comes before the verb in the sentence (go over the section **What are Objects?, p.** 148). If the direct object comes after the verb, there is no agreement and the past participle remains in its masculine singular form. Refer to your textbook which will go over this rule in detail. In the meantime, here are a few examples showing some structures where there is agreement.

Quelle **robe** as-tu **achetée**?

dir. obj.   past part.
  fem. sing.

*Which **dress** did you **buy?***

Quand avez-vous vu Marie? Je l'ai **vue** hier.

dir. obj. past part.
  fem. sing.

*When did you see Mary? I **saw her** yesterday.*

Voici le **manteau** et la **robe** que j'ai **achetés.**

antecedents   dir. obj.   past part.
    masc. pl.

*Here are the **coat** and the **dress** that I **bought.***

B. The Imperfect

The **imparfait** is a simple tense formed by adding certain endings to the stem of the verb. The conjugation is so regular that there is no need to repeat what is in your French textbook.

There are two English verb forms that indicate the **imparfait** should be used in French:

- if the English verb form includes, or could include, the helping verb *used to.*

    *When I was a child I **sang.***

    > *I sang* could be replaced by *used to sing;* therefore, the French verb is put in the **imparfait.**

    Quand j'étais petite je **chantais.**

    imparfait

- if the English verb form is in the past progressive tense, as in *was singing, were working.*

    *I **was singing** yesterday.*
    Je **chantais** hier.

    imparfait

Except for these two English verb forms, the English verb will not indicate to you whether you should use the **imparfait** or the **passé composé.**

IMPARFAIT OR *PASSÉ COMPOSÉ*

You will have to learn to analyze sentences and their context so that you can decide which of the two tenses to use.

For instance, let us consider the English sentence "Paul went out with Mary." The same form of the verb, namely "went out," is used in the two answers below, even though the verb has two different meanings:

1. QUESTION: What did Paul do yesterday?
    ANSWER: Paul went out with Mary.

    In this context, you are saying that Paul *went out* once with Mary. (The key word is *yesterday* in the question.)

2.   QUESTION: With whom did Paul go out when he was young?
     ANSWER: Paul went out with Mary.

In this context, you are saying that Paul *used to go out* with Mary.
(The key words are *when he was young* in the question.)

To translate "Paul went out with Mary" into French, you need to
know the context in which it is used (1 or 2 above), since the French
verb *went out* is in a different tense in each case.

> 1. Paul **est sorti** avec Marie.
>
> passé composé

> > Use of the **passé composé** implies that Paul went out
> > once with Mary.

> 2. Paul **sortait** avec Marie.
>
> imparfait

> > Use of the **imparfait** implies that Paul used to go out
> > with Mary or went out with her more than once.

Also, remember that since the **imparfait** and the **passé composé** both
take place at the same time in the past, these two tenses are often
used to compare the duration of one action to the duration of another
action in the same sentence or story. The **imparfait** is used for the
longer of the two actions. To help you choose the right tense, ask the
question "What happened?" The answer will require a verb in the
passé composé. The answer to the question "What was going on?"
will require a verb in the **imparfait**.

> *I was reading when he came in.*

> > Both actions are taking place at the same time, but the action of
> > *reading* was going on when the *coming in* happened.

> Je **lisais** quand il **est entré.**
>
> imparfait   passé composé

Your French textbook will give you additional guidelines to help you choose the appropriate tense. You should practice analyzing English paragraphs. Pick out the verbs in the past and indicate for each one if you would put it in the **imparfait** or in the **passé composé.** Sometimes both tenses are possible, but usually one of the two is more logical.

Practice

I. Fill in the blanks.

The (1) _____ and the (2) _____ are examples of the French past tense. The (3) _____ is a simple tense. The (4) _____ is composed of an auxiliary verb (5) _____ (*to have*) or (6) _____ (*to be*) conjugated in the (7) _____ tense plus the (8) _____ of the main verb.

II. The following is an important rule regarding the agreement of past participles in French.
- Fill in the blanks.
- Compare your answers to the Answer Key to make sure they are correct.
- Memorize the paragraph.

To establish the rules of agreement for a past participle, first look for the (1) _____ verb. If the auxiliary is (2) _____ , the past participle agrees in gender and number with the (3) _____ . If the auxiliary is (4) _____ , the past participle agrees in gender and number with the (5) _____ , if it comes before the (6) _____ .

III. The following are sentences in the past tense.
- Circle the verbs that would go in the **imparfait.**
- Box in the verbs that would go in the **passé composé.**

1. I went out a lot when I was going to college.

2. What were you doing in the car?

3. Peter called his friend from the airport.

4. Mary was talking to her friends when I saw her.

5. The students prepared their exam.

What is the Past Perfect?

The **past perfect tense** is used to express an action completed in the past before some other specific action or event occurred in the past. It is used when two actions happened at different times in the past and you want to indicate which action preceded the other.[1]

In English: The past participle is formed with the auxiliary **had** + the past participle of the main verb: *I had walked, he had seen,* etc.

She suddenly *remembered* that she *had forgotten* her keys.

past tense   past perfect

1   2

> Both action 1 and 2 occurred in the past, but action 2 preceded action 1. Therefore, action 2 is in the past perfect.

Don't forget that verb tenses indicate the time that an action occurs. Therefore, when verbs in the same sentence are in the same tense,

---

[1]You can compare this tense with the future perfect which is used when two actions will happen at different times in the future and you want to stress which action precedes the other (see **What is the Future Perfect?**, p. 94).

the actions took place during the same period of time. In order to show that they took place at different periods of time, different tenses must be used. Look at the following examples:

The car *was skidding* because it *was raining.*

past progressive
1

past progressive
2

Action 1 and action 2 took place at the same time.

The car *was skidding* because it *had rained.*

past progressive
1

past perfect
2

Action 2 took place before action 1.

In French: The past perfect is called **le plus-que-parfait.** It is formed with the auxiliary verb **avoir** or **être** in the **imparfait** + the past participle of the main verb: **j'avais marché, elle était allée.** The rules of agreement of the past participle are the same as for the **passé composé** (see pp. 82–83).

The **plus-que-parfait** is used to make clear that an action took place before an action in the **passé composé** or the **imparfait.**

In French and English the same relationship exists between the tense of the verb and the time when the action takes place.

Observe the sequence of events expressed by the past tenses in the following time-line:

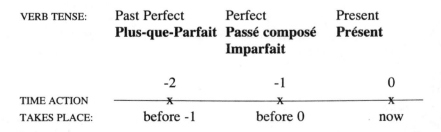

VERB TENSE:	Past Perfect	Perfect	Present
	Plus-que-Parfait	**Passé composé**	**Présent**
		Imparfait	
	-2	-1	0
TIME ACTION	x	x	x
TAKES PLACE:	before -1	before 0	now

- same verb tense = same time

  *The car **was skidding** because it **was raining**.*
  La voiture **dérapait** parce qu'il **pleuvait**.

  | imparfait | imparfait |
  | -1 | -1 |

  Two actions in the **imparfait** show that they took place at the same
  time in the past.

- different verb tenses = different times

  *The car **was skidding** because it **had rained**.*
  La voiture **dérapait** parce qu'il **avait plu**.

  | imparfait | plus-que-parfait |
  | -1 | -2 |

  The action in the **plus-que-parfait** (point -2) occurred before the
  action in the **imparfait** (point -1).

You cannot always rely on English to determine when to use the past
perfect. In many cases, English usage permits the use of the simple
past to describe an action that preceded another, if it is clear which
action came first.

  *The teacher **wanted** to know who **saw** the student.*

  | simple past | simple past |

  *The teacher **wanted** to know who **had seen** the student.*

  | simple past | past perfect |

  Although the two sentences above mean the same thing and are
  correct English, only the second sentence with its sequence of tenses
  would be correct in French.

Le professeur **voulait** savoir qui **avait vu** l'étudiant.

imparfait   plus-que-parfait
-1   -2

The verb in the **plus-que-parfait** (point -2) stresses that the action was completed before the action of "wanting to know" (point -1). In French the sequence of tenses is more rigid than in English.

Practice

Analyze the following sentences to determine the tenses of the verbs.
- In the parentheses, number the verbs according to the time line p. 88.
- On the line, write PP **(plus-que-parfait)** under the verbs that would take that tense.

1. Mary *read* the book she *saw* in the store yesterday.

    (-____)   (-____)

    _____   _____

2. When she *found* no money in her purse,

    (-____)

    _____

she *remembered* she *had gone* shopping.

    (-____)   (-____)

    _____   _____

3. Paul *wanted* to know who *called* him this morning.

    (-____)   (-____)

    _____   _____

Flashcards on a ring
A clear format
Visual clues

FRENCH IN THE PALM OF YOUR HAND™

■ Vocabulary compiled from today's first-year textbooks: ***Allons-y, Voilà, Invitation, Rendez-vous, Contacts,*** etc.

■ Not only the French word but *any* irregular forms of that word (irregular plurals, feminines, tenses, etc.)

■ Space for you to add French examples and to cross-reference to your textbook

■ English meaning, or meanings, with examples if needed

■ A booklet with a grammar review for each part of speech, study hints, and an alphabetical list of French and English words

What is the Future Tense?

The **future tense** indicates that an action will take place some time in the future.

In English: The future tense is formed with the auxiliary *will* or *shall* + the dictionary form of the main verb. Note that *shall* is used in very formal English (and British English), *will* occurs in everyday language.

> Paul and Mary *will do* their homework tomorrow.
> I *will leave* tonight.

In conversation, *shall* and *will* are often shortened to *'ll:* They'll do it tomorrow, I'll leave tonight.

In French: You do not need an auxiliary to show that the action will take place in the future. Future time is indicated by a simple tense.

Regular verbs use the infinitive as the stem for the future.

INFINITIVE	STEM	
aimer	aimer-	*to love*
finir	finir-	*to finish*
vendre	vendr-	*to sell*
	(the final "e" is dropped)	

Irregular verbs have irregular future stems which must be memorized.

INFINITIVE	STEM	
aller	ir-	*to go*
venir	viendr-	*to come*
avoir	aur-	*to have*
être	ser-	*to be*

You will notice that whatever the stem, regular or irregular, the sound of the letter "r" is always heard before the future ending. Your textbook will show you how to conjugate regular and irregular verbs in the future tense.

In many instances, French is more strict than English in its use of tenses. For example, while English uses the present tense after expressions such as *as soon as, when,* and *by the time,* which introduce an action that will take place in the future, French uses the future tense.

>*As soon as he **returns,** I will call.*
> |
>   present

>Dès qu'il **reviendra,** je téléphonerai.
> |
>   future
>"As soon as he will come . . ."

>*She will come when she **is** ready.*
> |
>   present

>Elle viendra quand elle **sera** prête.
> |
>   future
>". . . when she will be ready."

IMMEDIATE FUTURE

In English and in French the fact that an action will occur some time in the future can also be expressed without using the future tense itself, but a construction which implies the future.

In English: You can use the verb *to go* in the present progressive + the the dictionary form of the main verb: *I am going to walk, she is going to see,* etc.

>   similar meaning
>   ┌─────────────┴─────────────┐
>I *am going **to sing.**   I *will sing.*
> └─────┬─────┘
>present progressive
>of *to go* + infinitive

In French: The same construction exists in French. It is sometimes called **le futur immédiat** because the future action is considered nearer at hand than an action in the future tense. You can use the verb **aller** (*to go*) in the present tense + the infinitive of the main verb: **je vais marcher, elle va voir,** etc.

Je **vais chanter.**   Je **chanterai.**

present of **aller** + infinitive   future tense
immediate future

I *am going to sing*.   I *will sing*.

present of *to go* + infinitive   future tense
immediate future

In conversational French, **aller** + the infinitive often replaces the future tense.

Practice

I. The following are sentences with verbs in the future tense.
 • Circle the verbs.
 • On the line provided, write the dictionary form of the English verb you would put in the future tense in French.

DICTIONARY FORM

1. The students will study for their exam.   _____

2. I'll do my homework later.   _____

3. The Smiths will travel to France next summer.   _____

4. Will she attend the party with her friends?   _____

II. Indicate the tense of the verbs below.
- On line A indicate the tense as it is in the English sentence.
- On line B indicate the tense of the verb as it would be in a French sentence.

1. As soon as we *finish* our meal, we'*ll leave*.

   A. _____   _____

   B. _____   _____

2. We *will speak* French when we *go* to France this summer.

   A. _____   _____

   B. _____   _____

What is the Future Perfect?

The **future perfect tense** is used to express an action which will be completed in the future before some other specific action or event occurs in the future. It is used when two actions will happen at different times in the future and you want to indicate which action will come first.[1]

In English: The future perfect is formed with the auxiliary *will have* + the past participle of the main verb: *I will have walked, she will have gone,* etc.

I *will have finished* by the time school opens.
    └──────┬──────┘ └──────────┬──────────┘
      future perfect   future event
          1   2

---

[1]You can compare this tense to the past perfect which is used when two actions occurred at different times in the past and you want to stress which action preceded the other (see **What is the Past Perfect?,** p. 87).

Both action 1 and event 2 will occur at some future time, but action 1 will be completed before event 2 takes place. Therefore, action 1 is in the future perfect tense.

Before midnight, I *will have left*.

       future event   future perfect
           2   1

Both action 1 and event 2 will occur at some future time, but action 1 will be completed before event 2 takes place. Therefore, action 1 is in the future perfect tense.

In French: The future perfect is called **le futur antérieur.** It is formed with the auxiliary **avoir** or **être** in the future tense + the past participle of the main verb: **j'aurai marché, elle sera allée,** etc. The rules of agreement are the same as for the **passé composé** (see pp. 82–83).

The future perfect is used to express an action that will be completed in the future before some other specific action or event occurs in the future.

J'**aurai mangé** avant son arrivée.

     future perfect   future event
         1   2

I *will have eaten* before his arrival.

Action 1 will be completed before event 2 takes place. Therefore, action 1 is in the future perfect.

Avant minuit je **serai parti.**

     future event   future perfect
         2   1

*Before midnight I **will have left.***

Action 1 will be completed before event 2 takes place. Therefore, action 1 is in the future perfect.

Observe the sequence of events expressed by the future tenses in the following time-line:

VERB TENSE:	Present **Présent** 0	Future perfect **Futur antérieur** 1	Future **Futur** 2

TIME ACTION ————————x————————————x————————————x——
TAKES PLACE: now   after 0   after 0
                                      before 2

Future event 1 (the future perfect) precedes event 2 (the future); to use the future perfect you must have an event expressed in the future tense as a contrast, but you do not need an event in the present.

Compare these sentences:

This evening, the children will eat, go to bed, and then we will go out.
Ce soir, les enfants **mangeront** et **iront** au lit, et
                          | |
                        future   future
                          2   2

ensuite nous **sortirons.**
               |
             future
               2

All the verbs are in the future tense (2 on the time-line) because you are listing a series of things you are going to do in the future, "this evening."

This evening, we will go out after the children have eaten and gone to bed.
Ce soir, nous **sortirons** après que les enfants **auront mangé**
                  | └——————┬——————┘
               future   future perfect
                  2   1

et **se seront couchés.**
   └————————┬————————┘
      future perfect
            1

In French, the future perfect is required even though it is not used in English. Both the verbs in the future perfect (point 1) indicate that those actions will be accomplished before the action of "going out" (point 2). In French the sequence of tenses is more strict than in English.

Practice

Analyze the following sentences to determine the French tenses of the verbs.

- In the parentheses, number the verbs according to the time line p. 96.
- On the line below, write the French tense each verb would take.

1. When the bell *rings* at noon, they'*ll have finished* the exam.

      (___)   (___)

      _____   _____

2. As soon as I'*ve finished,* I'*ll call* him.

      (___)   (___)

      _____   _____

What is the Conditional?

The conditional mood does not exist in English, but is an important mood in French (see **What is Meant by Mood?**, p. 67). There is an English verb form however, which is similar to the French conditional and which can help you to understand it. For our purposes, we will call this form the "conditional."

In English: The "conditional" has a present and past tense.

A. PRESENT CONDITIONAL

The **present conditional** is a compound tense. It is formed with the auxiliary *would* + the dictionary form of the main verb.

> I said that I *would come* tomorrow.
> If she had the money, she *would call* him.
> I *would like* some ketchup, please.

Note: The auxiliary *would* in English has several meanings. It does not correspond to the conditional when it stands for *used to,* as in "She *would talk* while he painted." In this sentence, the verb means *used to talk* and requires the imperfect of the verb *to talk* in French (see p. 84).

The "present conditional" is used in the following ways:

1. in the main clause of a hypothetical statement

> If I had a lot of money, I *would buy* a Cadillac.

"I would buy a Cadillac" is called the **main clause, or result clause.** It is a clause because it is composed of a group of words containing a subject (*I*) and a verb (*would buy*) and is used as part of a sentence. It is the main clause because it expresses a complete thought and can stand by itself without being attached to the first part of the sentence ("If I had a lot of money"). It is called the result clause because it expresses what would happen as the result of getting a lot of money.

"If I had a lot of money" is called the **subordinate clause, or if-clause.** It is called subordinate because, although it contains a subject (*I*) and a verb (*had*), it does not express a complete thought and cannot stand alone. It must be attached to the main clause.

The entire statement is called **hypothetical** because it refers to a condition that does not exist at the present time (the person speaking does not have a lot of money), but there may be a remote possibility of its becoming a reality (the person speaking could have a lot of money one day).

2.   in an indirect statement to express a future-in-the-past

> He said Mary *would come*.
> (1)   (2)

"He said" is the main clause. The verb "said" prepares you for either a word-for-word quotation, called **direct speech,** or a summary of what was said, called **indirect speech.** "Mary would come" is an indirect statement (it summarizes what he said).

Action (1) is in the past and action (2) is to take place after, but still in the past. Action (2) is called a **future-in-the-past** because it takes place after another action in the past.

3.   as a polite form with *like* and in polite requests

> I *would like* to eat.
>
> > This is more polite than "I want to eat."
>
> *Would* you please close the door.
>
> > The command "please close the door" is softened by the use of *would*.

B. Past Conditional

The **past conditional** is formed with the auxiliary *would have* + the past participle of the main verb.

Unlike some statements in the present conditional where there is a possibility of their becoming a reality, all statements using the past conditional are **contrary-to-fact**: the main action never happened because the condition expressed was never met and it is now over and done with.

He *would have spoken* if he had known the truth.

Contrary-to-fact: He did not speak because he didn't know the truth.

If you had called us, we *would have come*.

Contrary-to-fact: We did not come because you didn't call us.

I *would have eaten* if I had been hungry.

Contrary-to-fact: I did not eat because I wasn't hungry.

In French: The conditional has a present and a past tense.

A. Present Conditional

You do not need an auxiliary to indicate the present conditional, **le conditionnel présent**; it is a simple tense. It is formed with the future stem (see p. 91) + the imperfect endings.

parler-	je parler**ais**	*I would speak*
finir-	je finir**ais**	*I would finish*
vendr-	je vendr**ais**	*I would sell*
aur-	j'aur**ais**	*I would have*
ser-	je ser**ais**	*I would be*

The present conditional is used in the following ways:

1. in the main clause of a hypothetical statement

Si j'avais beaucoup d'argent, j'**achèterais** une Cadillac.
present conditional

*If I had a lot of money, I **would buy** a Cadillac.*

2. in an indirect statement to express a future-in-the-past

Il a dit qu'il **viendrait.**
present conditional

*He said (that) he **would come.***

Je savais qu'il **pleuvrait.**
present conditional

*I knew (that) it **would rain.***

3. as a polite form or in polite requests

Je **voudrais** un sandwich.
present conditional

*I **would like** a sandwich.*

Voudriez-vous bien fermer la porte?
present conditional

***Would** you please close the door?*

B. Past Conditional

The past conditional, called **le conditionnel passé,** is formed with the auxiliary **avoir** or **être** in the present conditional + the past participle of the main verb: **j'aurais mangé, elle serait allée,** etc. As in English, all statements using the past conditional are contrary-to-fact.

Il **aurait parlé,** s'il avait su la vérité.
past conditional

*He **would have spoken,** if he had known the truth.*
past conditional

Sequence of Tenses

Let us study some examples of constructions with conditions and their results so that you learn to recognize them and to use the appropriate French tense.

Hypothetical and contrary-to-fact statements are easy to recognize because they are always made up of two clauses:

- the if-clause; that is, the subordinate clause that starts with *if* (**si** in French)
- the result clause; that is, the main clause

The sequence of tenses is the same in English and in French. If you have difficulty recognizing tenses just apply these three rules.

- if-clause = present tense / result clause = future tense

  If he comes, I shall be happy.
      present   future

  S'il **vient**, je **serai** contente.
      present   future

- if-clause = past tense / result clause = present conditional
           imparfait

  If he came, I would be happy.
      past   present conditional

  S'il **venait**, je **serais** contente.
      imparfait   present conditional

- if-clause = past perfect / result clause = past conditional

  If he had come, I would have been happy.
      past perfect   past conditional

  S'il **était venu**, j'**aurais été** contente.
      plus-que-parfait   past conditional

In English and in French the if-clause can come either at the beginning of the sentence before the main clause, or at the end of the sentence. The tense of each clause remains the same no matter the order.

Practice

Some of the verbs in the following sentences are in *italics*.
- For each of these verbs, identify the tense you would use in French by writing the appropriate letters on the lines provided: present (P), future (F) present conditional (PC), past conditional (PPC), **imparfait** (I), **plus-que-parfait** (PP).

1. Students *would do* their homework if they *had* time.

   _____   _____

2. If they *had had* an exam, they *would have studied*.

   _____   _____

3. Paul *would enjoy* meeting your parents.

   _____

4. When they *were* separated, he *would call* her every evening.

   _____   _____

5. They wrote me that they *would arrive* today.

   _____

6. We'*ll be going* abroad, if we *have* the money.

   _____   _____

What is a Reflexive Verb?

A **reflexive verb** is a verb that is linked to a special pronoun called a **reflexive pronoun;** this pronoun serves to "reflect" the action of the verb back to the performer, that is, to the subject of the sentence. The result is that the subject of the sentence and the object are the same person.

> *She* cut *herself* with the knife.
> *He* saw *himself* in the mirror.

In English: Many verbs can take on a reflexive meaning by adding a reflexive pronoun.

> Peter *cuts* the paper.
> regular verb

> Peter *cuts himself* when he shaves.
> verb + reflexive pronoun

Pronouns ending with *-self* or *-selves* are used to make verbs reflexive. Here are the reflexive pronouns.

	SUBJECT PRONOUN	REFLEXIVE PRONOUN
SINGULAR	I	myself
	you	yourself
	he	himself
	she	herself
	it	itself
PLURAL	we	ourselves
	you	yourselves
	they	themselves

In a sentence a reflexive pronoun is always tied to a specific subject, because both the pronoun and the subject refer to the same person or object.

I cut *myself.*
Paul and Mary blamed *themselves* for the accident.

Although the subject pronoun *you* is the same for the singular and plural, there is a difference between the reflexive pronouns used: *yourself* is used when you are speaking to one person (singular) and *yourselves* is used when you are speaking to more than one (plural).

Paul, did *you* make *yourself* a sandwich?
Children, make sure *you* dry *yourselves* properly.

In French: As in English many regular verbs can be turned into reflexive verbs by adding a reflexive pronoun.

Marie **lave** son enfant.
Mary washes her child.

Marie **se lave.**
Mary washes herself.

The dictionary lists **laver** as the infinitive of *to wash* and **se laver** as the infinitive of *to wash oneself.* Look up both forms under the verb **laver** and not under **se.**

Here are the French reflexive pronouns:

me	*myself*
te	*yourself* (familiar singular)
se	*himself, herself, itself*
nous	*ourselves*
vous	*yourselves* (familiar plural, formal singular & plural)
se	*themselves*

Since the reflexive pronoun reflects the action of the verb back to the performer, the reflexive pronoun will change as the subject of the verb changes. You will have to memorize the conjugation of reflexive verbs with the subject pronoun and the reflexive pronoun. For example, let's look at the conjugation of the verb **se laver** in the present tense. Notice that, unlike English, where the reflexive pronoun is placed after the verb, in French the reflexive pronoun is placed immediately before the verb.

SUBJECT PRONOUN	+	REFLEXIVE PRONOUN	+	VERB
je		me		lave
tu		te		laves
il elle		se		lave
nous		nous		lavons
vous		vous		lavez
ils elles		se		lavent

Reflexive verbs can be conjugated in all tenses. The subject pronoun and the reflexive pronoun remain the same, regardless of the tense of the verb: **je me laverai** (future); **ils se sont lavés (passé composé).** The perfect tenses of reflexive verbs are always conjugated with the auxiliary **être.** However, the rules of agreement for the past participle of reflexive verbs are different from the rules you apply to the past participles of non-reflexive verbs. Be sure to consult your French textbook for these rules.

Use of Reflexive Verbs

Reflexive verbs are more common in French than in English; that is, there are many verbs that take a reflexive pronoun in French but not in English. For example, when you say "Paul washed in the morning," it is understood, but not stated, that "Paul washed himself." In French the "himself" must be stated: "Paul **s'est lavé.**" In addition, other English verbs such as *to get up* have a reflexive meaning: "Mary got up" means that she got herself up. In French you express *to get up* by using the verb **se lever,** that is **lever** (*to raise*) + the reflexive pronoun **se** (*oneself*): "Marie **s'est levée.**" Memorize the many verbs that require a reflexive pronoun in French. Some of them are idiomatic expressions for which there is no direct equivalent in English.

Practice

I. Fill in the proper reflexive pronoun.

1. The children wash _____ every evening.

2. Mary always blames _____ .

3. Mary, you always blame _____ .

4. Children, behave _____ .

5. They do everything to suit _____ .

II. The following is a list of subject pronouns and the corresponding reflexive pronouns.

* Fill in the gaps on the lines provided.

	SUBJECT PRONOUN	REFLEXIVE PRONOUN
1.	il	_____
2.	nous	_____
3.	je	_____
4.	tu	_____
5.	vous	_____
6.	elles	_____

What is Meant by Active and Passive Voice?

The voice of the verb refers to a basic relationship between the verb and its subject. There are two voices:

The **active voice**—A sentence is said to be in the active voice when the subject is the performer of the verb. In this instance, the verb is called an **active verb.**

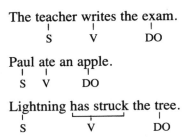

The teacher writes the exam.
  S   V   DO

Paul ate an apple.
 S   V   DO

Lightning has struck the tree.
 S   V   DO

In all these examples the subject (S) performs the action of the verb (V) and the direct object (DO) is the receiver of the action.

The **passive voice**—A sentence is said to be in the passive voice when the subject is the receiver of the action. In this instance, the verb is called a **passive verb.**

The exam is written by the teacher.
  S   V   Agent

The apple was eaten by Paul.
  S   V   Agent

The tree has been struck by lightning.
  S   V   Agent

In all these examples, the subject is having the action of the verb performed upon it. The performer of the action, if it is mentioned, is introduced by the word *by*. It is called the **agent.**

In English: The passive voice is expressed by the verb *to be* conjugated in the appropriate tense + the past participle of the main verb. The tense of the passive sentence is indicated by the tense of the verb *to be*.

The exam is written by the teacher.
        present

The exam was written by the teacher.
        past

The exam will be written by the teacher.
$\underbrace{\qquad\qquad}_{\text{future}}$

ACTIVE SENTENCE → PASSIVE SENTENCE

When an active sentence is changed into a passive sentence the following changes occur:

1. The direct object of the active sentence becomes the subject of the passive sentence.

ACTIVE:	The teacher writes *the exam.*
↓	direct object
PASSIVE:	*The exam* is written by the teacher.
	subject

2. The tense of the verb of the active sentence is reflected in the tense of the verb *to be* in the passive sentence.

ACTIVE:	The teacher *writes* the exam.
↓	present
PASSIVE:	The exam *is* written by the teacher.
	present

ACTIVE:	The teacher *wrote* the exam.
↓	past
PASSIVE:	The exam *was* written by the teacher.
	past

ACTIVE:	The teacher *will* write the exam.
↓	future
PASSIVE:	The exam *will be* written by the teacher..
	future

3. The subject of the active sentence becomes the agent of the passive sentence introduced with *by*. The agent is often omitted.

ACTIVE: *The teacher* writes the exam.
                          |
↓   subject

PASSIVE: The exam is written *by the teacher.*
                                                      |
                                                    Agent

In French: As in English, a passive verb is expressed by the auxiliary **être** (*to be*) conjugated in the appropriate tense + the past participle of the main verb. The tense of the passive sentence is indicated by the tense of the verb **être.**

L'examen **est** écrit par le professeur.
                  |
                present

The exam is written by the teacher.

L'examen **a été** écrit par le professeur.
                  └──┬──┘
                  passé composé

The exam was written by the teacher.

L'examen **sera** écrit par le professeur.
                  |
                future

The exam will be written by the teacher.

PRESENT PASSIVE OR *PASSÉ COMPOSÉ*

Be careful not to confuse a passive sentence in the present tense with an active sentence in the **passé composé.** For instance, "**a fermé**" is the **passé composé** of the verb **fermer** and "**est fermé**" is the present passive. As you can see below, the same changes occur in English.[1]

───────────────

[1]Verbs that take **être** as an auxiliary to form compound tenses in the active voice do not have a passive voice. For example, **aller, partir, venir,** etc. cannot be made passive.

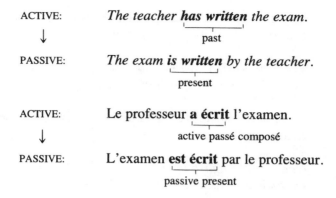

ACTIVE: *The teacher **has written** the exam.*
↓   past

PASSIVE: *The exam **is written** by the teacher.*
                              present

ACTIVE: Le professeur **a écrit** l'examen.
↓   active passé composé

PASSIVE: L'examen **est écrit** par le professeur.
                        passive present

Because the auxiliary is always **être** in the passive voice, all past participles agree in gender and number with the subject.

Les vins français sont appréciés dans le monde entier.
      | |
  masc. pl.   masc. pl.

*French **wines** are **appreciated** the world over.*

AVOIDING THE PASSIVE

Although French has a passive voice, it does not favor its use as English does, and whenever possible French speakers try to avoid the passive construction by replacing it with an active one. This is particularly true for general statements of this sort:

> English is spoken in many countries.
> The New York Times is sold here.

There are two ways a passive sentence can be avoided.

1. by using the **on** construction

The word **on** corresponds to the English indefinite pronoun *one*, as in the sentence, "One should eat when one is hungry." To avoid a passive construction, French often makes *one* the subject of an active sentence, even in sentences where English speakers would never use such a construction.

English *is spoken* in many countries.
One speaks English in many countries.

The New York Times *is sold* here.
One sells the New York Times here.

Once you have transformed the English passive sentence into the active form with *one,* write it in French.

One speaks English in many countries.
On parle anglais dans beaucoup de pays.

One sells the New York Times here.
On vend le New York Times ici.

2. by using the reflexive construction

To *reflect* the action back to the subject, the main verb of the sentence is written in its reflexive form (see **What is a Reflexive Verb?**, p. 104). This construction can only be used when the doer of the action (the agent) is unimportant and therefore not mentioned. This reflexive construction exists only in French and is usually senseless in English.

English *is spoken* in many countries.
"speaks itself"

The New York Times *is sold* here.
"sells itself"

Once you have replaced the English passive verb form with a reflexive verb, write it in French.

L'anglais **se parle** dans beaucoup de pays.
"speaks itself"

English is spoken in many countries.

Le New York Times **se vend** ici.

"sells itself"

*The New York Times **is sold** here.*

Practice

I. In the following sentences:
- Underline the subject of the sentence.
- Circle the performer of the action.
- Identify each sentence by writing "A" for active or "P" for passive on the line.

1. The cow jumped over the moon.   _____

2. The bill was paid by Bob's parents.   _____

3. The bank transfers the money.   _____

4. Everyone will be going away during the vacation. _____

5. The spring break will be enjoyed by all. _____

II. The following sentences are in the active voice.
- Underline the verb.
- Identify the tense of the verb by writing the appropriate letter on the line at the end of the sentence: Past (PP), Present (P), Future (F).
- Write the sentence in the passive voice on the line below.

1. All the students are taking the final exam.   _____

_____

_____

2. The teacher brought the children to the park.   _____

_____

_____

3. People all over the world will read that article. ⸻

⸻⸻⸻⸻⸻⸻⸻⸻⸻

⸻⸻⸻⸻⸻⸻⸻⸻⸻

What is the Subjunctive?

The **subjunctive** is a mood used to express a wish, hope, uncertainty or other similar attitude toward a fact or an idea. Since it stresses the speaker's feelings about the fact or idea, it is usually "subjective" about them.

In English: The subjunctive is used in only a very few constructions. The subjunctive verb form is difficult to recognize because it is spelled like other tenses of the verb.

> I *am* in Paris right now.
> indicative present *to be*

> I wish I *were* in Paris right now.
> subjunctive
> spelled like a past tense form of *to be*

> He *reads* a book a week.
> indicative present *to read*

> The course requires that he *read* a book a week.
> subjunctive
> spelled like the dictionary form of *to read*

The subjunctive occurs most commonly in the subordinate clause of three kinds of sentences:

1. The subjunctive of the verb *to be* (**were**) is used in conditional clauses introduced by *if*.

```
      if-clause              result clause
```
If I *were* in Europe now, I would go to Paris.

If Mary *were* more intelligent, she would learn faster.
                |
          subjunctive

2. The same subjunctive form **were** is used in statements expressing a wish that is not possible.

I wish I *were* in Europe right now.
          |
     subjunctive

I wish she *were* my teacher.
            |
       subjunctive

3. The subjunctive of any verb, which is the same as the dictionary form of that verb, is used in the clause following expressions of necessity or demand, often with verbs of asking, urging, demanding, and requesting.

It is necessary that he *be* here.
                        |
                   subjunctive

I asked that she *come* to see me.
                  |
             subjunctive

In French: The subjunctive is used very frequently, but unfortunately English usage will rarely help you decide where and how to use it in French. Therefore, we refer you to your French textbook. First, learn how to conjugate regular and irregular verbs in the present tense of the subjunctive. (The other tenses of the subjunctive are rarely used, particularly in conversation.) Then, learn the verbs and expressions that require you to put the verb which follows in the subjunctive.

1. Example of a verb of desire that is followed by a verb in the subjunctive: **vouloir** (*to want*)

   Je veux que tu **sois** sage.
   | |
   vouloir   subjunctive
              être

   *I want you **to be** good.*

   (Word-for-word: "I want that you should *be* good.")

2. Example of an expression that is followed by a verb in the subjunctive: **il faut que** (*it is necessary that*)

   Il faut que Paul **sache** parler français.
                      |
                  subjunctive
                  savoir

   *Paul must **know how** to speak French.*

   (Word-for-word: "It is necessary that Paul *know how* to speak French.")

3. Example of an adjective expressing an emotion which is followed by a verb in the subjunctive: **être heureux** (*to be happy*)

   Je suis heureuse que vous **veniez** ce soir.
                                |
                           subjunctive
                           venir

   *I am happy that you **are coming** this evening.*

Practice

None. Just study your textbook.

What is an Adjective?

An **adjective** is a word that describes a noun or a pronoun.

In English: Adjectives are classified according to the way they describe a noun or pronoun.

A **descriptive adjective** indicates a quality, it tells what kind it is. See p. 118.

> She read an *interesting* book.
> He has *brown* eyes.

A **possessive adjective** shows possession, it tells whose it is. See p. 122.

> *His* book is lost.
> *Our* parents are away.

An **interrogative adjective** asks a question about someone or something. See p. 127.

> *What* book is lost?
> *Which* parents did you speak to?

A **demonstrative adjective** points out someone or something. See p. 130.

> *This* teacher is excellent.
> *That* question is very appropriate.

In all these cases it is said that the adjective modifies the noun or pronoun.

In French: Adjectives as classified in the same way as in English. The principal difference between English and French adjectives is that in English adjectives do not change their form, while in French adjectives agree in gender and number with the noun or pronoun they modify.

Practice

Fill in the blanks.

An adjective is a word that describes a (1) _____ or a
(2) _____ , not a verb. An adjective that describes is
called a (3) _____ adjective. An adjective that tells
you whose it is, is called a (4) _____ adjective. An
adjective that asks a question about someone or something is called an
(5) _____ adjective and an adjective that points out
someone or something, is called a (6) _____ adjective.
The principal difference between English and French adjectives is that
French adjectives agree in (7) _____ and
(8) _____ with the word they modify, while English
adjectives don't change.

What is a Descriptive Adjective?

A **descriptive adjective** is a word that indicates a quality of a noun or
pronoun. As the name implies, it *describes* the noun or pronoun.

In English: The descriptive adjective does not change form, regardless
of the noun or pronoun it modifies.

> Mary is reading a *good* book.
> |
>   singular noun described

> Mary is reading *good* books.
> |
>   plural noun described

The adjective *good* is the same although in one instance it modifies a singular noun and in the other a plural noun.

Descriptive adjectives are divided into two groups depending on how they are connected to the noun they modify.

1. An **attributive adjective** is connected directly to its noun and always precedes it.

> The *good* children were praised.
> |
> noun described

> The family lives in a *small* house.
> |
> noun described

2. A **predicate adjective** is connected to its noun (the subject of the sentence) by a linking verb, usually a form of *to be*.

> The children are *good*.
> | | |
> noun   linking
> subject verb   predicate adjective

> The house looks *small*.
> | | |
> noun linking
> subject verb predicate adjective

NOUNS USED AS ADJECTIVES

You should also be able to recognize **nouns used as adjectives;** that is, a noun used to modify another noun.

> French is difficult.   The *French* class is crowded.
> | | |
> noun   adjective noun

> Chemistry is difficult.   The *chemistry* books are expensive.
> | | |
> noun   adjective noun

In French: The most important difference between descriptive adjectives in French and English is that in French they change forms. In French, an adjective, predicate and attributive, must always agree with the noun or pronoun it modifies; that is, it must correspond in gender and number to its noun. Thus, before writing an adjective you will have to determine if the noun or pronoun it modifies is masculine or feminine, singular or plural.

Most adjectives add an "**-e**" to the masculine form to make the feminine form and an "**-s**" to the feminine or masculine to make it plural.

*the **blue** book*	le livre **bleu**
	masc. masc.
	sing. sing.
*the **blue** dress*	la robe **bleue**
	fem. fem.
	sing. sing.
*the **blue** books*	les livres **bleus**
	masc. masc.
	pl. pl.
*the **blue** dresses*	les robes **bleues**
	fem. fem.
	pl. pl.

NOUNS USED AS ADJECTIVES

When a noun is used as an adjective, that is, to describe another noun, it remains a noun and does not change its form. Notice that a noun used as an adjective is introduced by the word **de.**

*the **French** class*	la **classe** de **français**
le français la classe	fem. masc.
	sing. sing.

the chemistry books   les **livres** de **chimie**

la chimie   les livres   masc.   fem.
                                   pl.   sing.

Practice

In the following sentences:
- Circle the adjectives.
- Draw an arrow from the adjective you circled to the noun or pronoun described.

1. The young man was reading a French newspaper.

2. She looked pretty in her red dress.

3. It is interesting.

4. The old piano could still produce good music.

5. Paul was tired after his long walk.

What is a Possessive Adjective?

A **possessive adjective** is a word which describes a noun by showing who "possesses" the thing or person being discussed. The owner is called the "possessor" and the noun modified is called the person or thing "possessed."

In English: Here is a list of the possessive adjectives:

	SINGULAR	
	1st PERSON	my
	2nd PERSON	your
	3rd PERSON	⎧ his ⎨ her ⎩ its
	PLURAL	
	1st PERSON	our
	2nd PERSON	your
	3rd PERSON	their

The possessive adjective refers only to the possessor and it does not agree in gender or number with the noun it modifies.

Paul's mother is young.   *His* mother is young.
  | |
possessor   person possessed

Mary's father is poor.   *Her* father is poor.
The cat's ears are short.   *Its* ears are short.

In French: Unlike English where possessive adjectives refer only to the possessor, French possessive adjectives refer to both the possessor and the possessed. Like all adjectives in French, the possessive adjective must agree in gender and number with the noun it modifies, that is, the person or object possessed.

For example, in the phrase **mon frère** (*my brother*) the first letter of the possessive adjective **m-** refers to the 1st person singular possessor *my*, while the ending **-on** is masculine singular to agree with **frère,** which is masculine singular. Let us see what happens when we make that phrase plural.

> *I love **my brothers**.*
> J'aime mes frères.
> ⌐┘
> masc.pl. endings
> 1st pers. sing.
> possessor

Mes refers to the possessor (*I, my*), but agrees in gender and number with the noun **frères.**

Here are the steps you should follow in choosing the correct possessive adjective:

A. MY, YOUR (**tu** form), HIS, HER, ITS

In French, each of these possessive adjectives has three forms: 1) the masculine singular, 2) the feminine singular, and 3) the plural (the same for both genders).

1. Indicate the possessor. This is shown by the first letter of the possessive adjective.

my	**m-**
your	**t-**
(**tu** form)	
his ⎫	
her ⎬	**s-**
its ⎭	

2. Fill in the possessive adjective so that it will agree in gender and number with the noun possessed. Start by analyzing the number of the noun possessed.

- If the noun possessed is singular, establish whether it is masculine or feminine.

  Add **-on** if the noun possessed is masculine, or if it is feminine beginning with a vowel.

Hélène lit **mon** livre.	*Helen reads **my** book.*
masc. sing.	
Hélène lit **ton** livre.	*Helen reads **your** book.*
Hélène lit **son** livre.	*Helen reads **her** (**his**) book.*

Paul rencontre **mon** amie.	*Paul meets **my** friend.*
fem. sing. begins with vowel	
Paul rencontre **ton** amie.	*Paul meets **your** friend.*
Paul rencontre **son** amie.	*Paul meets **his** (**her**) friend.*

  Add **-a** if the noun possessed is feminine beginning with a consonant.

Paul lit **ma** lettre.	*Paul reads **my** letter.*
fem. sing.	
Paul lit **ta** lettre.	*Paul reads **your** letter.*
Paul lit **sa** lettre.	*Paul reads **his** (**her**) letter.*

- If the noun possessed is plural, add **-es.**

Hélène lit **mes** livres.	*Helen reads **my** books.*
masc. pl.	
Paul lit **tes** lettres.	*Paul reads **your** letters.*
fem. pl.	
Elle lit **ses** livres.	*She is reading **her** (**his**) books.*
masc. pl.	

B. Our, Your (**vous** form), Their

In French, each of these possessive adjectives has only two forms: 1) the singular (the same for both genders), and 2) the plural (the same for both genders).

- If the noun possessed is singular, choose between **notre, votre, leur.**

> Marie est **notre** fille.   *Mary is **our** daughter.*
> Paul lit **votre** lettre.   *Paul reads **your** letter.*
> Ils lisent **leur** lettre.   *They read **their** letter.*

- If the noun possessed is plural, choose between **nos, vos, leurs.**

> Pierre et Marie sont **nos** enfants.   *Peter and Mary are **our** children.*
> Hélène lit **vos** livres.   *Helen reads **your** books.*
> Elles lisent **leurs** lettres.   *They read **their** letters.*

Before you write a sentence with *your*, decide whether it is appropriate to use the **tu** form or the **vous** form in French. Then make sure that every word that refers to "you" is in the right form, including the verb. "You are reading your letter" would be either **"Tu lis ta lettre"** or **"Vous lisez votre lettre."**

Note: In French and in English, the subject and the possessive adjective do not necessarily match. It all depends on what you want to say.

> Avez-**vous mon** livre?   *Do **you** have **my** book?*
>   2nd   1st   2nd   1st
>   pers.   pers.   pers.   pers.

Practice

I. In the following sentences:
- Circle the possessive adjective.
- Draw an arrow from the possessive adjective to the noun it modifies.

1. I took my exam home.

2. The Smiths now live in your house.

3. Paul looks like our mother.

4. Your clothes are expensive.

5. Paul put on his boots; Mary took her gloves, and they went out for

   their daily walk.

II. These are the steps to follow to choose the correct form of the French possessive adjectives.
- Fill in the missing elements in the blanks provided.

A. *My, your* (**tu** form), *his, her,* and *its:*

　1.　Indicate the _____ .

　　my = _____ -

　　your = _____ -
　　(**tu** form)

　　his
　　her = _____ -
　　its

　2.　Analyze the _____ of the noun possessed.

　　a)　The noun possessed is singular.

　　　If the noun possessed is _____ , or

　　　_____ starting with a vowel, add

　　　-_____ .

If the noun possessed is _____ beginning

with a consonant, add - _____ .

   b) The noun possessed is plural, add - _____ .

B. *Our, your (***vous*** form), and *their*

   1. If the noun possessed is singular, choose between

   _____ , _____ , and _____ .

   2. If the noun possessed is plural, choose between _____ ,

   _____ , and _____ .

What is an Interrogative Adjective?

An **interrogative adjective** is a word that asks a question about a noun.

In English: The words *which* and *what* are called interrogative adjectives when they come in front of a noun and are used to ask a question about that noun.

> *Which* teacher is teaching the course?
> *What* courses are you taking?

In French: There is one interrogative adjective **quel** which changes to agree in gender and number with the noun it modifies. Therefore, in order to say "which book" or "what dress" in French, you start by determining the gender and number of the word *book* or *dress*.

If the noun modified is masculine singular, use **quel.**

> ***What*** *book is on the table?*
>
> **Livre** (*book*) is masculine singular, so the word for "what" must be masculine singular.
>
> **Quel** livre est sur la table?
>   masc. sing.

If the noun modified is masculine plural, use **quels.**

> ***What*** *books are on the table?*
>
> **Livres** (*books*) is masculine plural, so the word for "what" must be masculine plural.
>
> **Quels** livres sont sur la table?
>   masc. pl.

If the noun modified is feminine singular, use **quelle.**

> ***What*** *dress are you wearing?*
>
> **Robe** (*dress*) is feminine singular, so the word for "what" must be feminine singular.
>
> **Quelle** robe portez-vous?
>   fem. sing.

If the noun modified is feminine plural, use **quelles.**

> ***What*** *dresses do you want?*
>
> **Robes** (*dresses*) is feminine plural, so the word for "what" must be feminine plural.
>
> **Quelles** robes voulez-vous?
>   fem. pl.

In the sentences above, the interrogative adjective immediately precedes the noun it modifies. This is not always the case. As you will see in the sentences below, the interrogative adjective is sometimes separated from the noun it modifies. You must learn to find that noun, because the interrogative adjective agrees with the noun it modifies no matter where it is placed in the sentence.

What *is your* **address?**

To establish which word the interrogative adjective modifies, the sentence can be restructured to read: "What address is yours?"

Quelle est votre **adresse?**

fem. sing.

What *are his favorite* **programs?**

To establish which word the interrogative adjective modifies, the sentence can be restructured to read: "What programs are his favorites?"

Quels sont ses **programmes** préférés?

masc. pl.

Note: The word *what* is not always an interrogative adjective. In the sentence *"What* is on the table?" it is an interrogative pronoun. It is important that you distinguish one from the other, because different words are used here in French and they follow different rules. (See **What is an Interrogative Pronoun?**, p. 171.)

Practice

I. In the following sentences:
- Circle the interrogative adjective.
- Draw an arrow from the interrogative adjective to the noun it modifies.

1. Which class are you going to?

2. Please tell me what exercises are due tomorrow?

3. Which hotel are you staying at?

4. Which is your favorite restaurant?

II. In the following sentences:
- Circle the English interrogative adjectives.
- Fill in the blanks.

1. Which dresses are you taking to France?

    Robes (in English: _____) is feminine plural.

    _____ robes apportes-tu en France?

2. What is your trade?

    Métier (in English: _____) is masculine singular.

    _____ est ton métier?

What is a Demonstrative Adjective?

A **demonstrative adjective** is a word used to point out a person or an object.

In English: The demonstrative adjectives are *this* and *that* in the singular and *these* and *those* in the plural. They are rare examples of adjectives agreeing in number with the noun they modify: *this* changes to *these* and *that* changes to *those* when they modify a plural noun.

SINGULAR	PLURAL
this cat	*these* cats
that man	*those* men

This and *these* refer to a person or object near the speaker, and *that* and *those* refer to a person or object away from the speaker.

In French: There is only one demonstrative adjective **ce** which changes to agree in gender and number with the noun it modifies. Therefore, in order to say "that book" or "that dress" in French, you start by determining the gender and number of the word *book* or *dress*.

If the noun modified is masculine singular and starts with a consonant, use **ce.**

>*This* (or *that) book is on the table.*
>
>>**Livre** (*book*) is masculine singular, so the word for "this" must be masculine singular.
>
>**Ce** livre est sur la table.
>└─┬─┘
>masc. sing.

If the noun modified is masculine singular and starts with a vowel, use **cet.**

>*This* (or *that) apartment is large.*
>
>>**Appartement** (*apartment*) is masculine singular. Since it begins with a vowel, the word for "this" must be **cet.**
>
>**Cet** appartement est grand.
>└──┬──┘
>   masc. sing.
>   noun begins with vowel

If the noun modified is feminine singular, use **cette.**

>*This* (or *that) dress is pretty.*
>
>>**Robe** (*dress*) is feminine singular, so the word for "this" must be feminine singular.
>
>**Cette** robe est jolie.
>└──┬──┘
> fem. sing.

If the noun modified is plural, use **ces.**

These (or *those) books are on the table.*

Livres (*books*) is masculine plural, so the word for "those" must be masculine plural.

Ces livres sont sur la table.

masc. pl.

These (or *those) dresses are pretty.*

Robes (*dresses*) is feminine plural, so the word for "these" must be feminine plural.

Ces robes sont jolies.

fem. pl.

Practice

I. In the following sentences:
- Circle the demonstrative adjective.
- Draw an arrow from the demonstrative adjective to the noun it modifies.

1. They prefer that restaurant.

2. This test is too hard.

3. You paid too much for those books.

4. These houses are more expensive than those.

II. In the following sentences:
- Circle the demonstrative adjective.
- Fill in the blanks.

1. That lesson is too difficult for me.

    1. Gender of noun modified: feminine

    2. Number of noun modified: _____

    _____ leçon est trop difficile pour moi.

2. This hotel is not expensive.

    1. Gender of noun modified: masculine

    2. Number of noun modified: _____

    _____ hôtel n'est pas cher.

3. These restaurants are expensive.

    1. Gender of noun modified: masculine

    2. Number of noun modified: _____

    _____ restaurants sont chers.

What is Meant by Comparison of Adjectives?

We compare adjectives when two or more nouns have the same quality, and we want to indicate that one of these nouns has a greater, lesser, or equal degree of this quality.

comparison of adjectives

Paul is tall but Mary is taller.

adjective   adjective

modifies *Paul*   modifies *Mary*

There are two types of comparison: comparative and superlative.

In English: Let us go over what is meant by the different types of comparison and how each type is formed.

1. The **comparative** compares a quality of one person or thing with the same quality in another person or thing. The comparison can indicate that one or the other has more, less, or the same amount of the quality.

The comparison of greater degree (more) is formed:

- short adjective + *-er* + *than*

    Paul is tall*er than* Mary.
    Mary is pretti*er than* her sister.

- *more* + longer adjective + *than*

    Paul is *more* intelligent *than* Mary.
    My car is *more* expensive *than* your car.

The comparison of lesser degree (less) is formed:

- *not as* + adjective *as,* or *less* + adjective + *than*

    Paul is *not as* tall *as* Mary.
    My car is *less* expensive *than* your car.

The comparison of equal degree (same) is formed:

- *as* + adjective + *as*

    Paul is *as* tall *as* Mary.
    My car is *as* expensive *as* your car.

2. The **superlative** is used to stress the highest and lowest degrees of a quality.

The superlative of highest degree is formed:

• *the* + short adjective + *-est*

  Mary is *the* pretti*est*.
  My car is *the* cheap*est* on the market.

• *the most* + long adjective

  Mary is *the most* intelligent.
  His car is *the most* expensive of all.

The superlative of lowest degree is formed:

• *the least* + adjective

  Mary is *the least* stupid.
  His car is *the least* expensive of all.

A few adjectives do not follow this regular pattern of comparison. You must use an entirely different form for the comparative and the superlative.

ADJECTIVE:	This apple is *good*.
COMPARATIVE:	This apple is *better*.
	not "gooder"
SUPERLATIVE:	This apple is the *best*.
	not "goodest"

In French: There are the same two types of comparison of adjectives as in English: comparative and superlative. Remember that agreement between the adjective and the noun is always required.

1. The comparative is formed by adding **plus** (*more*), or **moins** (*less*), or **aussi** (*as*) + adjective + **que**

   Paul est **plus** intelligent **que** Marie.
   *Paul is **more** intelligent **than** Mary.*

Ma voiture est **moins** chère **que** votre voiture.
*My car is **less** expensive **than** your car.*

Marie est **aussi** jolie **que** sa soeur.
*Mary is **as** pretty **as** her sister.*

2. The superlative is formed by **le, la,** or **les** (depending on the gender and number of the noun described) + **plus** (*most*) or moins (*least*) + adjective.

Marie est **la plus** jolie de la famille.
     └──┬──┘
       fem. sing.

*Mary is **the prettiest** in the family.*

Paul est **le plus** grand.
     └──┬──┘
      masc. sing.

*Paul is **the tallest**.*

Marie et Paul sont **les plus** intelligents de la classe.
└────┬────┘
     masc. pl.

*Mary and Paul are **the most** intelligent in the class.*

Ma voiture est **la moins** chère.
     └──┬──┘
      fem. sing.

*My car is **the least** expensive.*

As in English, a few adjectives have irregular forms of comparison which you will have to memorize individually.

| ADJECTIVE: | Cette pomme est **bonne.** |
| | *This apple is **good**.* |

| COMPARATIVE: | Cette pomme est **meilleure.** |
| | *This apple is **better**.* |

SUPERLATIVE: Cette pomme est **la meilleure**.
This apple is the best.

Note: Adverbs (see **What is an Adverb?**, p. 138) are compared in the same manner as adjectives in both English and French.

Practice

I. Using the elements given, write sentences with comparative adjectives. The various degrees of comparison are indicated as follows:

    + + superlative   = equal degree
    + greater degree   - lesser degree

1. The teacher is / (+) old / the students.

———————————————————————————

2. He is / (-) intelligent / I am.

———————————————————————————

3. Mary is / (=) tall / Paul.

———————————————————————————

4. That boy is / (+ +) bad / in the school.

———————————————————————————

5. Paul is a / (+) good student / Mary.

———————————————————————————

II. If you had to translate the following sentences into French, you would have to determine whether to use **le, la,** or **les** to form the superlative.
   • Circle the noun you would have to analyze.

1. Paul wrote the best composition.

2. She did the least difficult exercises.

3. Mary is certainly the most attractive girl in the class.

4. Paul is the most diligent and least talkative student.

What is an Adverb?

An **adverb** is a word that describes a verb, an adjective, or another adverb. Adverbs indicate quantity, time, place, intensity, and manner.

> Mary drives *well*.
> |
>   verb

> The house is *very* big.
> |
>   adjective

> The girl ran *too* quickly.
> |
>   adverb

In English: Here are some examples of adverbs:

- of quantity or degree

    > Mary sleeps *little* these days.
    > Paul does *well enough* in class.

    These adverbs answer the question *how much?*

- of time

    > He will come *soon*.
    > The children arrived *late*.

    These adverbs answer the question *when?*

- of place

    > The teacher looked *around*.
    > The old were left *behind*.

    These adverbs answer the question *where?*

* of intensity

> These are *really* beautiful.
> Mary can *actually* read Latin.

These adverbs are used for *emphasis*.

* of manner

> Mary sings *beautifully*.
> They parked the car *carefully*.

These adverbs answer the question *how?* They are the most common adverbs and can usually be recognized by their *-ly* ending.

In French: You will have to memorize most adverbs as vocabulary items. Most adverbs of manner can be recognized by the ending **-ment** which corresponds to the English ending *-ly*.

joli**ment**	*beautifully*
générale**ment**	*generally*
heureuse**ment**	*happily*

The most important fact for you to remember is that adverbs are **invariable:** this means that they never change their form. (Adverbs never become plural, nor do they have gender.)

ADVERB OR ADJECTIVE

Because adverbs are invariable and adjectives must agree with the noun they modify, you must be able to distinguish one from the other. When you write a sentence in French, always make sure that adjectives agree with the nouns or pronouns they modify and that adverbs remain unchanged.

*The **tall** girl talked **rapidly**.*

Tall modifies the noun *girl;* it is an adjective. *Rapidly* modifies the verb *talked;* it describes how she talked; it is an adverb.

La **grande** fille parlait **rapidement**.
　　fem. sing.　　　　adverb

*The **tall** boy talked **rapidly**.*

Tall modifies the noun *boy;* it is an adjective. *Rapidly* modifies the verb *talked;* it describes how he talked; it is an adverb.

Le **grand** garçon parlait **rapidement**.
　　masc. sing.　　　　adverb

Remember that in English *good* is an adjective; *well* is an adverb.

The student writes *good* English.

Good modifies the noun *English;* it is therefore an adjective.

The student writes *well*.

Well modifies the verb *writes;* it is therefore an adverb.

Likewise, in French **bon** is an adjective meaning *good;* **bien** is the adverb meaning *well*.

*The **good** students speak French **well**.*
　adjective　　　　　　　adverb

Les **bons** étudiants parlent **bien** le français.
　masc. pl.　　　　　　adverb

Adverbs are compared in the same manner as adjectives (see **What is Meant by Comparison of Adjectives?**, p. 133).

Practice

In the following sentences:
- Circle the adverbs.
- Draw an arrow from the adverb to the word it modifies.

1. The students arrived early.
2. Paul learned the lesson really quickly.
3. The students were too tired to study.
4. He has a reasonably secure income.
5. Mary is a good student who speaks French very well.

What is a Conjunction?

A **conjunction** is a word that links words or groups of words.

In English: There are two kinds of conjunctions: coordinating and subordinating.

1. **Coordinating conjunctions** join words, phrases, and clauses that are equal; they *coordinate* elements of equal rank. The major coordinating conjunctions are *and, but, or, nor, for,* and *yet.*

   good *or* evil
   over the river *and* through the woods
   They invited us, *but* we couldn't go.

2. **Subordinating conjunctions** join a dependent clause to a main clause; they *subordinate* one clause to another. A clause introduced by a subordinating conjunction is called a **subordinate clause.** Typical subordinating conjunctions are *before, after, since, although, because, if, unless, so that, while, that,* and *when.*

Although we were invited, we didn't go.

subordinating   main
conjunction   clause

They left *because* they were bored.

main   subordinating
clause conjunction

He said *that* he was tired.

main   subordinating
clause conjunction

Notice that the subordinate clause may come either at the beginning of the sentence or after the main clause.

In French: Conjunctions must be memorized as vocabulary items. Remember that, like adverbs and prepositions, conjunctions are invariable (i.e., they never change their form).

Practice

In the following sentences:
- Circle the coordinating and subordinating conjunctions.
- Underline the words each conjunction serves to coordinate or to subordinate.

1. Mary and Paul were going to study French or Spanish.

2. She did not study because she was too tired.

3. Not only had he forgotten his ticket, but he had forgotten his passport as well.

4. She knew he was mean, yet she still loved him.

5. They borrowed money so they could go to France.

What is a Preposition?

A **preposition** is a word that shows the relationship of one word (usually a noun or pronoun) to another word in the sentence. The noun or pronoun following the preposition is called the **object of the preposition.** The preposition plus its object is called a **prepositional phrase.** Prepositions normally indicate position, direction, or time.

In English: Here are examples of some prepositions showing:

* position

> Paul was *in* the car.
> Mary put the books *on* the table.

* direction

> Mary went *to* school.
> The students came directly *from* class.

* time

> French people go on vacation *in* August.
> *Before* class, they went to eat.

Not all prepositions are single words:

because of	in front of	instead of
due to	in spite of	on account of

In French: You will have to memorize prepositions as vocabulary items. Their meaning and use must be carefully studied. There are three important things to remember:

1. Prepositions are invariable. This means that they never change their form. (They never become plural, nor do they have a gender.)

2. Prepositions are tricky little words. Every language uses prepositions differently. Do not assume that the same preposition is used
in French as in English, or even that a preposition will be used
in French when you must use one in English (and vice versa).

ENGLISH   FRENCH
          CHANGE OF PREPOSITION
to be angry *with*   être fâché **contre** (*against*)
to be *on* the plane   être **dans** (*in*) l'avion

PREPOSITION   →   NO PREPOSITION
to wait *for*   attendre
to look *at*   regarder

NO PREPOSITION   →   PREPOSITION
to telephone   téléphoner **à**
to ask (someone)   demander **à**

A good dictionary will usually give you the verb plus the preposition when one is required. In particular, be careful not to translate
an English verb + preposition word-for-word. For example,
when you consult the dictionary to find the French equivalent of
look for, do not stop at the first entry for *look* (which is **regarder**)
and then add the preposition **pour** (corresponding to *for*). Continue searching for the specific meaning *look for* (which corresponds to the verb **chercher** used without a preposition).

> *I am looking for Peter.*
> Je **cherche** Pierre.

On the other hand, when looking up a verb such as *enter,* be sure
to include the French preposition **dans** which you find listed in
the entry.

> *Mary is entering the classroom.*
> Marie **entre dans** la salle de classe.

3. Although the position of a preposition in an English sentence may vary, it cannot in French. Spoken English often places a preposition at the end of the sentence; in this position it is called a **dangling preposition**. In formal English there is a strong tendency to avoid dangling prepositions by placing them within the sentence or at the beginning of a question.

SPOKEN ENGLISH	→	FORMAL ENGLISH
The man I spoke *to* is French.		The man *to whom* I spoke is French.
Who are you playing *with?*		*With whom* are you playing?
Here is the girl you asked *about.*		Here is the girl *about whom* you asked.

French places prepositions the same way as formal English, that is, within the sentence or at the beginning of a question. A preposition is never placed at the end of a French sentence.

L'homme **à qui** j'ai parlé.
*The man **to whom** I spoke.*

Avec qui joues-tu?
With whom are you playing?

There are some English expressions where the natural position of the preposition is at the end of the sentence; it is not a question of the difference in spoken or formal language.

They don't understand what he is talking *about.*

Changing the structure by placing the preposition within the sentence would sound awkward.

They don't understand *about what* he is talking.

However, as awkward as it may sound in English, this is the structure that must be used in the French sentence:

Ils ne comprennent pas **de quoi** il parle.
*They do not understand **about what** he is talking.*

Preposition *De*

A special word needs to be said about the French preposition **de** (*of, some, etc.*) because it is used in many French constructions.

1. When a noun is used as an adjective to describe another noun (see p. 119), **de** is used as follows:

   - the noun described + **de** + the describing noun used without an article

A	B	B	A
le livre **de** chimie		*the chemistry book*	
la classe **de** français		*the French class*	
l'huile **d'**olive		*the olive oil*	

   The noun in Column B describes the noun in Column A. Notice how the describing noun comes after **de** and the described noun in French, while it comes before the described noun in English.

2. When indicating the quantity of a noun, **de** is used as follows:

   - the quantity + **de** + the noun without an article

une douzaine **d'**oeufs	*a dozen eggs*
une livre **de** beurre	*a pound of butter*
beaucoup **d'**étudiants	*many students*

3. When a noun possesses another noun (see p. 25) **de** is used as follows:

   - the noun possessed + **de** + definite or indefinite article + the noun that possesses

A	B	B	A

le sac **de la** dame   *the lady's handbag*

les branches **d'un** arbre   *a tree's branches*

la bicyclette **du** garçon   *the boy's bicycle*

$\boxed{\text{de + le}}$

le club **des** filles   *the girls' club*

$\boxed{\text{de + les}}$

The noun in Column A belongs to the noun in Column B. Notice how the possessed noun comes before the possessor in French, while it comes after in English. The French structure parallels the English structure *the handbag of the lady, the branches of a tree, the bicycle of the boy,* and *the club of the girls.*

Practice

I. Circle the prepositions in the following sentences.

1. The students didn't understand what the lesson was about.

2. The waiter had come from Paris the year before.

3. The teacher walked around the room as she talked.

4. Contrary to popular opinion he was a good student.

5. The garden between the two houses was very small.

II. The following are sentences in informal English.
*   On the line below each sentence, write the restructured sentence that parallels the structure of a French sentence.

1. I know what he was speaking about.

_____

2. Who are you explaining the grammar to?

_____

3. Who are you making the dress for?

_____

What are Objects?

Every sentence consists, at the very least, of a subject and a verb. This is called the **sentence base.**

Children play.
Work stopped.

The subject of the sentence base is usually a noun or pronoun. Many sentences contain other nouns or pronouns which are related to the action of the verb or to a preposition. These nouns or pronouns are called **objects.**

Paul writes a letter.
subject | object
        verb

He speaks to Mary.
subject | object
        verb

Paul goes out with Mary.

subject | | object
verb preposition

There are three types of objects:

1. direct object
2. indirect object
3. object of a preposition

1. AND 2. DIRECT AND INDIRECT OBJECTS

In English: Let us see how these two types of objects are identified in English.

1. **direct object:** It is a noun or pronoun that receives the action of the verb directly, without a preposition. It answers the question *what?* or *whom?* asked after the verb.[1]

> Paul writes *a letter.*
>
> > Paul writes what? A letter.
> > *A letter* is the direct object.

> They see *Paul and Mary.*
>
> > They see whom? Paul and Mary.
> > *Paul and Mary* are the two direct objects.

Do not assume that any word which comes right after a verb is automatically the direct object. It must answer the question *what?* or *whom?*

> Paul sees well.
>
> > Paul sees *what?* No answer.
> > Paul sees *whom?* No answer.

There is no direct object in the sentence. *Well* is an adverb; it answers the question: Paul sees *how?*

---

[1] In this section, we will consider active sentences only. See **What is Meant by Active and Passive Voice?**, p. 107).

2. **indirect object:** It is a noun or pronoun which receives the action of the verb indirectly with the preposition *to* relating it to the verb. It answers the question *to what?* or *to whom?* asked after the verb.

> She spoke *to her friends.*
>
>> She spoke to whom? Her friends.
>> *Her friends* is the indirect object.

> He gave the painting *to the museum.*
>
>> He gave a painting to what? The museum.
>> *The museum* is the indirect object.

A sentence may contain both a direct object and an indirect object. In English, when both objects are present, the indirect object usually precedes the direct object, but without the preposition *to.*

> Paul gave *his sister* a gift.
>
>> *His sister* answers the question *to whom?* and is the indirect object in the sentence, even though the preposition "to" does not appear.

When a sentence has both a direct and an indirect object, the following two word orders are possible:

- subject (S) + verb (V) + indirect object (IO) + direct object (DO)

> Paul gave his sister a gift.
> | | | |
>   S   V   IO   DO
>
>> *Who* gave a gift? Paul.
>> *Paul* is the subject.
>>
>> Paul gave *what?* A gift.
>> *A gift* is the direct object.
>>
>> Paul gave a gift *to whom?* His sister.
>> *His sister* is the indirect object.

- subject + verb + direct object + *to* + indirect object

Paul gave a gift to his sister.
S   V   DO   IO

Note that although the word order changes, the function of each word does not. Be sure that you ask the questions to establish the functions of the words in a sentence.

In French: Direct and indirect objects are related to the verb in the same way they are in English. However, indirect objects are easier to identify because they are always preceded by the preposition **à**. So those objects not preceded by a preposition are always direct objects.

1. Direct object = no preposition separates it from the verb.

   Paul prend **le livre.**
   *Paul takes **the book.***

   Ils rencontrent **Paul et Marie.**
   *They meet **Paul and Mary.***

2. Indirect object = the preposition **à** separates it from the verb.

   Paul parle **à son frère.**
   *Paul speaks **to his brother.***

   Il écrit **au professeur.**
   | à + le |
   *He writes **to the teacher.***

When a sentence contains both a direct and an indirect object, the direct object always precedes the indirect object. There is only one word order possible when the objects are nouns (pronoun objects follow a different word order):

- subject + verb + direct object + à + indirect object

Paul a donné un cadeau à sa soeur.

    S   V   DO   IO

*Paul gave **his sister** a gift.*
*Paul gave a gift **to his sister**.*

3. OBJECT OF A PREPOSITION

In English: An object of a preposition is a noun or pronoun which is related to a preposition other than *to*. (Objects of the preposition *to* are discussed under indirect objects above.) It answers the question *what?* or *whom?* asked after the preposition.

Paul went *with Mary.*

> With whom? With Mary.
> *Mary* is the object of the preposition *with*.

He is working *for Mr. Jones.*

> For whom? For Mr. Jones.
> *Mr. Jones* is the object of the preposition *for*.

In French: An object of a preposition is as easy to identify as in English. It follows a preposition other than **à** (*to*).

Marie vient **avec Paul.**
*Mary comes **with Paul**.*

Il travaille **pour M. Jones.**
*He works **for Mr. Jones**.*

OBJECTS IN ENGLISH AND FRENCH

The relationship between verb and object are often different in English and French. For example, a verb may take an object of a preposition in English but a direct object in French, or a direct object in English but an indirect object in French. For this reason, it is important that you pay close attention to such differences when you learn French verbs. Your textbook, as well as dictionaries, will indicate when a French verb is followed by a preposition.

Here are some examples of the kinds of differences that you are most likely to encounter.

• Object of a preposition in English → Direct object in French

> *I am looking **for the book**.*
>
> > Function in English: Object of a preposition
> > For what? The book.
> > *The book* is the object of the preposition *for*.
>
> Je cherche **le livre**.
>
> > Function in French: Direct object
> > Je cherche quoi? Le livre.
> > Since **chercher** is not followed by a preposition, it takes a direct object.

Here is a list of a few common verbs that require an object of a preposition in English but a direct object in French.

*to look **for***	chercher
*to look **at***	regarder
*to wait **for***	attendre
*to pay **for***	payer
*to listen **to***	écouter

• Direct object in English → Indirect object in French

> *She phones **her friends** every day.*
>
> > Function in English: Direct object
> > Whom does she phone every day? Her friends.
> > *Her friends* is the direct object.
>
> Elle téléphone **à ses amis** tous les jours.
>
> > Function in French: Indirect object
> > A qui téléphone-t-elle tous les jours? A ses amis.
> > The verb is **téléphoner à** and takes an indirect object.

Here is a list of a few common verbs that require a direct object in English and an indirect object in French.

to call, telephone	téléphoner **à**
to obey	obéir **à**
to resemble	ressembler **à**

- Direct object in English → Object of a preposition in French

   *Mary's parents remember **the war**.*

   > Function in English: Direct object
   > Mary's parents remember what? The war.
   > *The war* is the direct object.

   Les parents de Marie se souviennent **de la guerre.**

   > Function in French: Object of preposition
   > De quoi se souviennent les parents de Marie? De la guerre.
   > The verb is **se souvenir de** and it requires an object for the preposition **de.**

Here is another common verb which requires a direct object in English and an object of a preposition in French.

to enter	entrer **dans**

Always identify the function of a word within the language in which you are working; do not mix English patterns into French.

SUMMARY

The different types of objects in a sentence can be identified by looking to see if they are introduced by a preposition and, if so, by which one.

An object which receives the action of the verb directly, without a preposition, is called direct.

An object which receives the action of the verb indirectly, through the preposition *to*, is called indirect.

An object which is related to a preposition other than *to* is called object of a preposition.

Your ability to recognize the three kinds of objects is essential when using pronouns. For example, different pronouns are used for the English pronoun *him* depending on whether *him* is a direct object (**le**) or an indirect object (**lui**).

Practice

Find the objects in the following sentences:
- Next to Q, write the question you need to ask to find the object.
- Next to A, write the answer to the question you just asked.
- In the column to the right, identify the kind of object it is by circling the appropriate letters: Direct object (DO), Indirect object (IO), or Object of a preposition (OP).

1. The children took a shower.

    Q: _____

    A: _____   DO   IO   OP

2. They ate the meal with pleasure.

    Q: _____

    A: _____   DO   IO   OP

    Q: _____

    A: _____   DO   IO   OP

3. He sent a present to his brother.

    Q: _____

    A: _____   DO   IO   OP

    Q: _____

    A: _____   DO   IO   OP

4. The parents paid for the books with a credit card.

Q: _____

A: _____   DO   IO   OP

Q: _____

A: _____   DO   IO   OP

What is an Object Pronoun?

An **object pronoun** is a pronoun used as an object of a verb or a preposition.

In English: Pronouns change according to their function in the sentence. Pronouns used as subjects are studied in **What is a Subject Pronoun?**, p. 45. We use subject pronouns when we learn to conjugate verbs (see **What is a Verb Conjugation?**, p. 51). In this section we shall look at pronouns used as objects. Object pronouns are used when a pronoun is either a direct object, indirect object, or object of a preposition. (See **What are Objects?**, p. 148.)

> She saw *me*.
> |
> direct object = object pronoun

> I lent my car to *him*.
> |
> indirect object = object pronoun

> They went out with *her*.
> |
> object of a preposition = object pronoun

Compare the subject and object pronouns:

	SUBJECT	OBJECT
SINGULAR		
1st PERSON	I	me
2nd PERSON	you	you
	he	⎧ him
3rd PERSON	she	⎬ her
	it	⎩ it
PLURAL		
1st PERSON	we	us
2nd PERSON	you	you
3rd PERSON	they	them

The form of the object pronoun is the same whether the pronoun is used as a direct object, indirect object, or an object of a preposition.

In French: Different object pronouns are used for each kind of object: direct, indirect, and object of a preposition. You will therefore have to learn how to analyze them and how to choose the correct French form.

A. DIRECT AND INDIRECT OBJECT PRONOUNS

In French it is easier to distinguish between direct and indirect objects with nouns rather than with pronouns, because nouns that are indirect objects are always preceded by the preposition à, while pronouns are not. Often a different form of the pronoun is used for the direct and indirect object.

Let us look at each of the English pronouns and see how to find the French equivalent.

1. 1st and 2nd persons singular and plural (*me, you,* and *us*)

The French equivalents have the same forms when they are used as direct and indirect object pronouns.

	SUBJECT	DIRECT AND INDIRECT OBJECT
SINGULAR		
1st PERSON	je	me
2nd PERSON	tu	te
PLURAL		
1st PERSON	nous	nous
2nd PERSON	vous	vous

Once you have established that a 1st or 2nd person pronoun is either a direct or indirect object, you merely have to place the correct form of the pronoun in front of the conjugated French verb.

*Paul sees **me**.*
      |
      Paul sees whom? Me.
      Me is the direct object pronoun.

Paul **me** voit.
   |
direct object pronoun

*Paul speaks **to me**.*
      |
      Paul speaks to whom? Me.
      Me is the indirect object pronoun.

Paul **me** parle.
   |
indirect object pronoun

The fact that **nous** and **vous** can be either the subject or the object in a sentence is sometimes confusing, particularly since both subject and object pronouns are placed before the verb in French. It is important that you do not think of these pronouns only as subjects. In case of doubt, look at the verb. Remember that verbs agree with their subject. If **nous** is the subject, the verb will end in **-ons;** if it doesn't, **nous** is an object of some kind. The same is true with **vous.** If it is the subject of the verb, the ending of regular verbs will be **-ez.**

Le professeur **nous** regarde.

Nous cannot be the subject because the verb **regarde** doesn't end in **-ons.** The subject of **regarde** can only be **le professeur.** Therefore, **nous** must be an object pronoun.

The teacher looks at us.

Le professeur **vous** parle.

Vous cannot be the subject because the verb **parle** doesn't end in **-ez.** The subject of **parle** can only be **le professeur.** Therefore, **vous** must be an object pronoun.

The teacher speaks to you.

2. 3rd person singular and plural (*him, her, it,* and *them*)

The French equivalents have a different form depending on whether they are used as direct or indirect objects. When the pronoun is a direct object, a different form is used depending on the gender and number of the pronoun. When the pronoun is an indirect object, a different form is used depending on whether its antecedent refers to a "Person" (this category includes human beings and live animals) or a "Thing" (this category includes objects and ideas).

	SUBJECT	DIRECT OBJECT	INDIRECT OBJECT	
ANTECEDENT:	PERSON AND THING		PERSON	THING
SINGULAR				
MASCULINE	il	le	lui	y
FEMININE	elle	la	lui	y
PLURAL				
MASCULINE	ils	les	leur	y
FEMININE	elles	les	leur	y

An analysis of the following sentences, in which we have used each of the 3rd person English object pronouns, will enable us to select the proper French form from the chart above.

Him–Always masculine singular; refers to a person. You will only have to determine whether this pronoun is a direct or indirect object.

> *Do you see Paul? Yes, I see **him**.*
>> 1. Function : direct object
>> You see whom? Him.
>> 2. Selection: **le**

Voyez-vous Paul? Oui, je **le** vois.

> *Are you giving Paul the book? Yes, I am giving **him** the book.*
>> 1. Function: indirect object
>> You give the book to whom? Him.
>> 2. Selection: **lui**

Donnez-vous le livre à Paul? Oui, je **lui** donne le livre.

Her–Always feminine singular; refers to a person. You will only have to determine whether this pronoun is a direct or indirect object.

> *Do you see Mary? Yes, I see **her**.*
>> 1. Function: direct object
>> You see whom? Her.
>> 2. Selection: **la**

Voyez-vous Marie? Oui, je **la** vois.

> *Are you giving the book to Mary? Yes, I am giving **her** the book.*
>> 1. Function: indirect object
>> You give the book to whom? Her.
>> 2. Selection: **lui**

Donnez-vous le livre à Marie? Oui, je **lui** donne le livre.

Note: The only way you can tell if **lui** refers to a male or female is from what has been said before.

It–Always singular; always refers to a thing. You will have to determine whether this pronoun is a direct or indirect object. If it is a direct object, you will have to determine whether its antecedent is masculine or feminine. (Don't forget that *it* can also be the subject of a sentence; see **What is a Subject Pronoun?**, p. 45.)

> *Do you see the book? Yes, I see it.*
>
>   1. Function: direct object
>   You see what? It.
>   2. Antecedent: **Le livre** (*the book*) is masculine.
>   3. Gender: masculine
>   4. Selection: **le**

Voyez-vous le livre? Oui, je **le** vois.

> *Do you see the table? Yes, I see it.*
>
>   1. Function: direct object
>   You see what? It.
>   2. Antecedent: **La table** (*the table*) is feminine.
>   3. Gender: feminine
>   4. Selection: **la**

Voyez-vous la table? Oui, je **la** vois.

> *Are you answering the letter? Yes, I am answering it.*
>
>   1. Function: indirect object
>   **Répondre à** (*to answer*) takes an indirect object.
>   2. Selection: **y**

Répondez-vous à la lettre? Oui, j'**y** réponds.

Them–Always plural; refers to persons and things. You will have to determine whether this pronoun is a direct or indirect object. If it is an indirect object, you will have to determine whether its antecedent refers to persons or things.

> *Do you see the children? Yes, I see them.*
>
>   1. Function: direct object
>   You see whom? The children.
>   2. Selection: **les**

Voyez-vous les enfants? Oui, je **les** vois.

*Did you give Paul and Mary the book? Yes, I gave **them** the book.*

1. Function: indirect object
   I gave the book to whom? Paul and Mary.
2. Type of antecedent: persons (*Paul and Mary*)
3. Selection: **leur**

Avez-vous donné le livre à Paul et à Marie? Oui, je **leur** ai donné le livre.

*Do you obey your parents? Yes, I obey **them**.*

1. Function: indirect object
   Obéir à (*to obey*) takes an indirect object.
2. Type of antecedent: persons (*parents*)
3. Selection: **leur**

Obéissez-vous à vos parents? Oui, je **leur** obéis.

*Do you obey the laws? Yes, I obey **them**.*

1. Function: indirect object
   Obéir à (*to obey*) takes an indirect object.
2. Type of antecedent: things (*laws*)
3. Selection: **y**

Obéissez-vous aux lois? Oui, j'**y** obéis.

B. Pronouns as Objects of Prepositions

Pronouns that are objects of prepositions other than *to* have certain forms which are different from the forms used as direct objects and indirect objects. Unlike other object pronouns which are placed before the verb, pronouns as objects of prepositions are usually placed, with the preposition, after the verb. In this they are like nouns used as objects of prepositions. (The pronoun **en** is an exception to this rule, see below under 2.)

Let us look at each of the English pronouns and see how to find the French equivalent.

1.   1st and 2nd persons singular and plural (*me, you,* and *us*)

	SUBJECT	DIRECT AND INDIRECT OBJECT	OBJECT OF PREPOSITION
SINGULAR			
1st PERSON	je	me	moi
2nd PERSON	tu	te	toi
PLURAL			
1st PERSON	nous	nous	nous
2nd PERSON	vous	vous	vous

Once you have established that a 1st or 2nd person pronoun is an object of a preposition, you merely have to write down the preposition and the correct pronoun after the conjugated French verb.

*Is the book for Paul? No, it's for **me**.*
*No, it's for **you**.*
*No, it's for **us**.*

1. Function: object of preposition *for*
2. Selection : **moi**
   toi or **vous**
   nous

Est-ce que le livre est pour Paul? Non, il est pour **moi**.
Non, il est pour **toi**
(*or* **vous**).
Non, il est pour **nous**.
|
object of preposition
pour

2.   3rd person singular and plural (*him, her, it,* and *them*)

The French equivalents have a different form depending on the gender and number of the pronoun. You will also have to determine whether the antecedent is a person or a thing. If the antecedent is a thing, a different pronoun is used if the preposition is **de**.

ANTECEDENT:	SUBJECT	DIRECT OBJECT	INDIRECT OBJECT		OBJECT OF PREPOSITION	
	PERSON AND THING		PERSON	THING	PERSON (after all prep.) THING (after all prep. besides **de**)	THING[1] (after **de**)
SINGULAR MASCULINE	il	le	lui	y	lui	en
FEMININE	elle	la	lui	y	elle	en
PLURAL MASCULINE	ils	les	leur	y	eux	en
FEMININE	elles	les	leur	y	elles	en

An analysis of the following sentences, in which we have used each of the 3rd person English pronouns objects of prepositions, will enable us to select the proper French form from the chart above.

Him–Always masculine singular; *her* always feminine singular. You only have to establish whether these pronouns are objects of a preposition.

> *Is the book for Paul? Yes, it is for **him**.*
> *Is the book for Mary? Yes, it is for **her**.*

      1. Function: object of preposition *for*
      2. Selection: **lui**
                elle

Est-ce que le livre est pour Paul? Oui, il est pour **lui**.
Est-ce que le livre est pour Marie? Oui, il est pour **elle**.
                                     |
                             object of preposition
                             pour

It–Always singular; refers to a thing. In French, a noun referring to a thing is not replaced by a pronoun when it follows a preposition other than **de.** (For instance, one does not say "The book is on *it*" referring to *the table;* instead one says "The book is on *the table.*") When *it* is the object of the preposition **de,** both the preposition and the pronoun are replaced by **en** which is placed before the verb.

---

[1]Your textbook may cover the few cases in which the pronoun **en** can be used to refer to persons.

I liked the book so I am going to speak about it.

1. Function : object of the preposition **de** (*about*)

J'ai aimé le livre alors je vais **en** parler.

de + object of preposition

Them–Always plural; refers to persons and things. A different object pronoun is used if the antecedent is a person or thing. If the antecedent is a person, you will have to determine the gender of its antecedent. If the antecedent is a thing, *them* is not used after a preposition other than **de** (see explanation under *it* above). When *them* is the object of the preposition **de,** both the preposition and the pronoun are replaced by **en** which is placed before the verb.

Are you going out with the girls? Yes, I'm going out with them.

1. Function: object of preposition **avec** (*with*)
2. Type of antecedent: persons (*girls*)
3. Antecedent: **Les filles** (*the girls*) is feminine.
4. Selection: **elles**

Allez-vous sortir avec les filles? Oui je vais sortir avec **elles.**

object of preposition
avec

Are you going with the children? No, I'm going without them.

1. Function: object of preposition **sans** (*without*)
2. Type of antecedent: persons (*children*)
3. Antecedent: **Les enfants** (*the children*) is masculine.
4. Selection: **eux**

Allez-vous avec les enfants? Non, je vais sans **eux.**

object of preposition
sans

Paul has two daughters. He always speaks about **them.**

1. Function: object of the preposition **de** (*about*)
2. Type of antecedent: persons (*girls*)
3. Gender: **Les filles** (*the girls*) is feminine.
4. Selection: **elles**

Paul a deux filles. Il parle tout le temps d'**elles.**
                                              |
                                    object of preposition
                                    de

I liked these books so I am going to speak **about them.**

1. Function: object of the preposition **de** (*about*)
2. Type of antecedent: things (*books*)
3. Selection: **en**

J'ai aimé ces livres alors je vais **en** parler.
                                    |
                        de + object of preposition

DISJUNCTIVE (STRESSED) PRONOUNS

The set of pronouns used as objects of prepositions has another function. These pronouns are also used for emphasis or contrast. In this function, they are called **disjunctive** or **stressed pronouns.** Disjunctive pronouns often stand alone.

Who is there? **Him.**
             Her.
               |
           personal pronoun
           standing alone

Qui est là? **Lui.**
           Elle.
             |
        disjunctive pronoun

Who called? **Me.**
              |
          personal pronoun
          standing alone

Qui a téléphoné? **Moi.**
                  |
             disjunctive pronoun

SUMMARY

Below is a flow chart of the steps you have to follow to find the French equivalent of each English object pronoun. It is important that you do the steps in sequence, because each step depends on the previous one.

DO = Direct object in the French sentence
IO = Indirect object in the French sentence
OP = Object of a preposition or disjunctive pronoun
in the French sentence

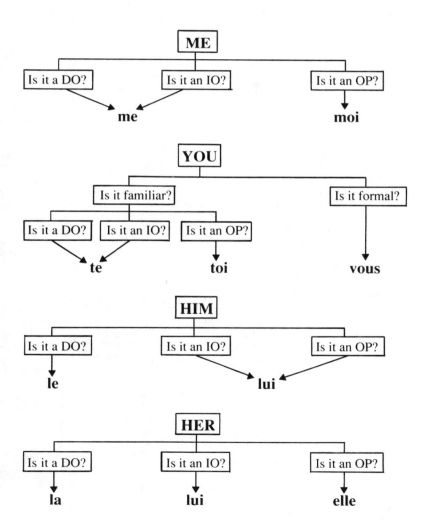

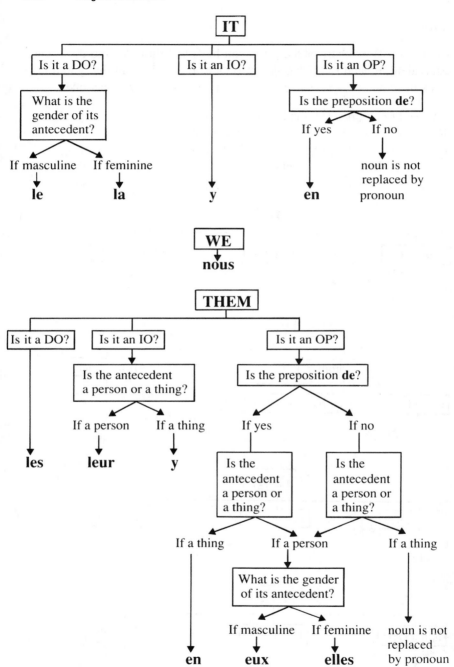

Practice

I. In the following sentences:
- Underline the object pronoun.
- Circle the letters which correspond to its function in the sentence: Direct object (DO), Indirect object (IO), or Object of a preposition (OP).

1. He bought it with the money he had earned. DO IO OP

2. Mary went with him to the movies. DO IO OP

3. She lifted the book and placed the letter under it. DO IO OP

4. The children saw me leaving. DO IO OP

5. The teacher gave us the exam today. DO IO OP

6. The radio was given to you as a present. DO IO OP

II. In the following sentences:
- Circle the English object pronoun.
- Fill in the steps you must follow to choose the correct French form (see pp. 167–8).
- Using the charts in this section, fill in the French object pronoun in the French sentence below.

1. Paul drives her in the old car.

    1. Function of pronoun : _____

    Paul _____ conduit dans la vieille voiture.

2. Mary likes the book and she takes it.

    1. Function of pronoun : _____
    2. Antecedent : _____
    3. Gender : masculine

    Marie aime le livre et elle _____ prend.

3. The teacher spoke to them about the exam yesterday.

   1. Function of pronoun: _____
   2. Type of antecedent : _____

Le professeur _____ a parlé de l'examen hier.

4. Did you answer his letters? No, we will answer them today.

   1. Function of pronoun: _____
   Remember *to answer* is **répondre à.**

   2. _____ : Not persons.

Avez-vous répondu à ses lettres? Non, nous _____ répondrons aujourd'hui.

5. Go with her.

   1. Function of pronoun: _____

Va avec _____ .

6. Robert and Paul are going to Paris and I am going with them.

   1. Function of pronoun: _____
   2. Is it the object of the preposition **de** (*of*): _____
   3. Antecedents : _____
   4. Gender: _____

Robert et Paul vont à Paris et je vais avec _____ .

7. Who is there? Me.

   1. Function of pronoun: _____

Qui est là? _____.

8. Paul doesn't like exams. He is afraid of them.

    1. Function of pronoun: _____
     Remember *to be afraid of* is **avoir peur de.**
    2. _____ : Yes.
    3. Type of antecedent: _____

Paul n'aime pas les examens. Il _____ a peur.

What is an Interrogative Pronoun?

An **interrogative pronoun** is a word that replaces a noun and introduces a question. Interrogative comes from *interrogate,* to question.

In English: Different interrogative pronouns are used depending on whether you are referring to a "Person" (this category includes human beings and live animals) or a "Thing" (this category includes objects and ideas). Also, the interrogative pronoun referring to persons changes according to its function in the sentence.

A. PERSONS

Who is used for the subject of the sentence.

    Who lives here?
     |
    subject

    Who are they?
     |
    subject

Whom is used for the direct object, indirect object, and the object of a preposition.

> **Whom** do you know here?
> |
> direct object

> To **whom** did you speak?
> |
> indirect object

> From **whom** did you get the book?
> |
> object of preposition *from*

In informal English, *who* is often used instead of *whom*, and prepositions are placed at the end of the sentence, separated from the interrogative pronoun to which they are linked.

> *Who* do you know here?
> |
> instead of *whom*

> *Who* did you speak *to?*
> | |
> instead of *whom*   preposition

> *Who* did you get the book *from*?
> | |
> instead of *whom*   preposition

Whose is the possessive form and is used to ask about possession or ownership.

> *Whose* pencil is this?
> |
> possessive

> They are nice cars. *Whose* are they?
> |
>   possessive

B. THINGS

What refers only to things, and the same form is used for subject, direct object, indirect object, and the object of a preposition.

What happened?
|
subject

What do you want?
|
direct object

What do you cook with?
|
object of preposition *with*

In French: A different interrogative pronoun is used depending on whether the pronoun replaces a person or a thing. Also, the interrogative pronoun changes according to its function in the sentence. Look at the different forms in this chart.

	SUBJECT	DIRECT OBJECT	INDIRECT OBJECT AND OBJECT OF PREPOSITION
	who	*who(m)*	preposition + *who(m)*
PERSON	qui est-ce qui qui	qui est-ce que qui + inversion	prep. + qui est-ce que prep. + qui + inversion
	what	*what*	prep. + *what*
THING	qu'est-ce qui	qu'est-ce que que + inversion	prep. + quoi est-ce que prep. + quoi + inversion

To choose the correct form, proceed with the following two steps:

1. Determine the function of the interrogative pronoun in the sentence (subject, direct object, indirect object, or object of a preposition).
2. Establish whether the pronoun refers to a person or a thing.

Refer to the chart above as we look at an example of each form.

A. SUBJECT

Refers to a person: **qui** or **qui est-ce qui** (*who*)

Who speaks French?
|
subject of *speaks*

Qui parle français?
Qui est-ce qui parle français?

Refers to a thing: **qu'est-ce qui** (*what*)

What is on the table?
|
subject of *is*

Qu'est-ce qui est sur la table?

B. DIRECT OBJECT

Refers to a person—**Qui est-ce que** or **qui** + inversion

Who(m) do you see?
|
direct object of *see*
(*You* is the subject.)

Qui est-ce que vous voyez?
Qui voyez-vous?
        └─┬─┘
       inversion

Refers to a thing: **qu'est-ce que** or **que** + inversion

What do you want?
|
direct object of *want*
(*You* is the subject.)

Qu'est-ce que vous voulez?
Que voulez-vous?
        └─┬─┘
       inversion

C. Indirect Object and Object of a Preposition

In an English sentence, it is sometimes hard to decide whether a pronoun is an indirect object or an object of a preposition. To make it easier for you to identify these two functions you should change the sentence from the word order of spoken English to the word order of formal English. All you have to do is place the preposition before the pronoun. This restructure will not only make it easier for you to identify the function of the pronoun, but it will also establish the French word order. (See p. 145.)

The following sentences have been restructured to avoid a dangling preposition.

Who are you giving the book *to?* →
| |
pronoun   preposition

To whom are you giving the book?
|
indirect object

What are you contributing *to?* →
| |
pronoun   preposition

To what are you contributing?
|
indirect object

Who are you going out *with?* →
| |
pronoun   preposition

With whom are you going out?
|
object of the preposition *with*

What are you writing *with?* →
| |
pronoun   preposition

With what are you writing?
|
object of the preposition *with*

Now that you have established the function of the interrogative pronoun, you only have to establish whether the pronoun refers to a person or a thing.

Refers to a person: preposition + **qui est-ce que**
preposition + **qui** + inversion

> ***To whom** are you giving the book?*
> |
> indirect object
> (*Book* is the direct object.)

A qui est-ce que vous donnez le livre?
A qui donnez-vous le livre?
⌞‾‾‾⊤‾‾‾⌟
inversion

> ***With whom** are you going out?*
> |
> object of preposition *with*

Avec qui est-ce que vous sortez?
Avec qui sortez-vous?
⌞‾‾⊤‾‾⌟
inversion

Refers to a thing: preposition + **quoi est-ce que**
preposition + **quoi** + inversion

> ***To what** are you contributing?*
> |
> indirect object

A quoi est-ce que vous contribuez?
A quoi contribuez-vous?
⌞‾‾‾⊤‾‾‾⌟
inversion

> ***With what** are you writing?*
> |
> object of the preposition *with*

Avec quoi est-ce que vous écrivez?
Avec quoi écrivez-vous?
⌞‾‾‾⊤‾‾‾⌟
inversion

Once again we remind you that some French verbs take direct objects, while the equivalent English verbs take an indirect object and vice-versa. Make sure that you determine the function of the pronoun in French.

"WHICH ONE," "WHICH ONES"

There is another interrogative pronoun which we will now examine separately because it does not follow the same pattern as the ones above.

In English: *Which one, which ones* can refer to both persons and things; they are used in questions that request the selection of one (*which one,* singular) or several (*which ones,* plural) from a group. The words *one* and *ones* are often omitted. These interrogative pronouns may be used as a subject, direct object, indirect object, and object of a preposition.

All the teachers are here. *Which one* teaches French?

singular subject

I have two cars. *Which one* do you want to take?

singular direct object

There are many children here. With *which ones* do you want to speak?

plural object of the preposition *with*

In French: These interrogative pronouns do not change according to their function. They change according to the gender of their antecedent, and their number depends on whether you want to say *which* **one** (singular) or *which* **ones** (plural). Here they are:

	SINGULAR	PLURAL
MASCULINE	lequel	lesquels
FEMININE	laquelle	lesquelles

To choose the proper form, follow these steps:

1. Determine the antecedent.
2. Determine the gender of the antecedent.
3. Determine the number: *one* is singular and *ones* is plural.
4. Select the correct French form from the above chart.

Let us apply these steps to some examples.

> *All the teachers are here. **Which one** teaches French?*
>
> 1. Antecedent: *the teachers*
> 2. Gender: **Un professeur** (*a professor*) is masculine.
> 3. Number: *One* is singular.
> 4. Selection: **lequel**

Tous les professeurs sont ici. **Lequel** enseigne le français?

> *I have two cars. **Which one** do you want to take?*
>
> 1. Antecedent: *the cars*
> 2. Gender: **Une voiture** (*a car*) is feminine.
> 3. Number: *One* is singular.
> 4. Selection: **laquelle**

J'ai deux voitures. **Laquelle** veux-tu prendre?

> *There are many children here. With **which ones** do you want to play?*
>
> 1. Antecedent: *children*
> 2. Gender: **Les enfants** (*the children*) is masculine.
> 3. Number: *Ones* is plural.
> 4. Selection: **lesquels**

Il y a beaucoup d'enfants ici. Avec **lesquels** veux-tu jouer?

> *Here are four girls; **which ones** do you want to speak to?*
>
> Restructure: Place the preposition before the interrogative pronoun.

*Here are four girls; **to which ones** do you want to speak?*

1. Antecedent: *girls*
2. Gender: **Une fille** (*a girl*) is feminine.
3. Number: *Ones* is plural.
4. Selection: **lesquelles**

Voici quatre filles; **auxquelles** voulez-vous parler?

| à + lesquelles = auxquelles |

*There are two books. **Which one** are you speaking about?*

Restructure: Place the preposition before the interrogative pronoun.

*There are two books. **About which one** are you speaking?*

1. Antecedent: *books*
2. Gender: **Un livre** (*a book*) is masculine.
3. Number: *One* is singular.
4. Selection: **lequel**

Il y a deux livres. **Duquel** parlez-vous?

| de + lequel = duquel |

Practice

I. In the following sentences:
- Circle the interrogative pronoun.
- Fill in the steps you must follow to choose the correct French form.
- Using the chart in this section, fill in the French interrogative pronoun in the French sentences below.

1. Who came into the room?

    1. Function of pronoun: _____

    2. Type of antecedent : _____

    _____ est entré dans la pièce?

2. Who are you going with?

    1. Function of pronoun: _____

    2. Type of antecedent : _____

Avec _____ allez-vous?

3. What did you put it under?

    1. _____ : _____

    2. _____ : _____

Sous _____ l'avez-vous mis?

4. Who did you call?

    1. _____ : _____

    2. _____ : _____

_____ est-ce que vous avez appelé?

5. What is she doing tonight?

    1. _____ : _____

    2. _____ : _____

_____ fait-elle ce soir?

II. The following are sentences with the expressions *which one* and *which ones*.
- Fill in the steps you have to follow to choose the correct French equivalent.
- Using the chart in this section, fill in the French equivalent in the French sentences below.

1. There are the two skirts I bought. Which one do you want?

    1. Antecedent: _____

    2. Gender : feminine

    3. Number: _____

    Voilà les deux jupes. _____ veux-tu?

2. I bought a lot of books. Which ones do you want to read?

    1. _____ : _____

    2. _____ : masculine

    3. _____ : _____

    J'ai acheté beaucoup de livres. _____ voulez-vous lire?

3. Paul has many sisters. Which one did you go out with?

    1. _____ : _____

    2. _____ : _____

    3. _____ : _____

    Paul a beaucoup de soeurs. Avec _____ es-tu sorti?

What is a Demonstrative Pronoun?

A **demonstrative pronoun** is a word that replaces a noun previously mentioned, **the antecedent,** as if pointing to it. Demonstrative comes from *demonstrate,* to show.

In English: The singular demonstrative pronouns are *this (one)* and *that (one)*; the plural forms are *these* and *those.*

> Here are two suitcases. *This one* is big and *that one* is small.

> The books are on the shelves. *These* are in French, *those* in English.

As with the demonstrative adjectives, *this (one)/these* refer to a person or an object near the speaker, and *that (one)/those* to a person or an object away from the speaker.

In French: Demonstrative pronouns do not change with function, but they agree in gender and number with their antecedent; **-ci** is added to indicate objects closer to the speaker and **-là** to indicate objects farther away.

	SINGULAR	PLURAL
MASCULINE	celui	ceux
FEMININE	celle	celles

To choose the correct form, follow these steps:

1. Determine the antecedent.
2. Determine the gender and number of the antecedent.
3. Based on steps 1 and 2 choose the correct form from the chart.
4. Add **-ci** for *this* or *these* and **-là** for *that* and *those.*

Look at the following examples.

Give me the book. ***This one.***

1. Antecedent: book
2. Gender & number: **Le livre** (*the book*) is masculine singular.
3. Selection: **celui**
4. *This* = **-ci**

Donne-moi le livre. **Celui-ci.**
masc. sing.

Give me the letter. ***That one.***

1. Antecedent: letter
2. Gender & number: **La lettre** (*the letter*) is feminine singular.
3. Selection: **celle**
4. *That* = **-là**

Donne-moi la lettre. **Celle-là.**
fem. sing.

Give me the books. ***These.***

1. Antecedent: books
2. Gender & number: **Les livres** (*the books*) is masculine plural.
3. Selection: **ceux**
4. *These* = **-ci**

Donne-moi les livres. **Ceux-ci.**
masc. pl.

Give me the letters. ***Those.***

1. Antecedent: letters
2. Gender & number: **Les lettres** (*the letters*) is feminine plural.
3. Selection: **celles**
4. *Those* = **-là**

Donne-moi les lettres. **Celles-là.**
fem. pl.

"THE ONE," "THE ONES"

There is another demonstrative pronoun which we will now examine separately because it does not follow the same pattern as the ones above.

In English: The demonstrative pronouns *the one* and *the ones,* unlike *this one* and *that one,* do not point out a specific object, but instead introduce a clause that helps us identify an object by giving additional information about it. There is a singular form *the one* and a plural form *the ones.* They are often followed by the relative pronoun *that* or *which* (see **What is a Relative Pronoun?**, p. 196).

> What book are you reading?
> I am reading *the one (that)* I bought yesterday.

> > Clause: *the one that I bought yesterday* gives us additional infor-
> > mation about *the book.* Notice that the relative pronoun
> > *that* can be omitted in English.
> > Number: *The one* is singular.

> Which dresses do you prefer?
> I prefer *the ones that* are in front.

> > Clause: *the ones that are in front* gives us additional information
> > about *the dresses.*
> > Number: *The ones* is plural.

In French: The demonstrative pronouns corresponding to *the one* and *the ones* agree in gender and number with the antecedent. The relative pronoun *that* or *which* is selected according to its function in the relative clause (see pp. 196–99). The relative pronoun that can be omitted in English must be stated in French.

To choose the correct form, follow these steps:

> Demonstrative pronoun (*the one, the ones*)
> 1. Find the antecedent.
> 2. Determine the gender and number of the antecedent.
> 3. Select the correct French form from the chart on p. 182.
> Relative pronoun (*that, which*—add it to the English sentence if
> it has been omitted)
> 1. Determine the function of the relative pronoun in the rela-
> tive clause.
> 2. Select the correct French form:
> - the subject of the relative clause = **qui**
> - the object of the relative clause = **que**

A good way to check that you have chosen the correct form is that **qui** is always followed by a verb.

Let us apply these rules to the following examples:

What book are you reading?
*I'm reading **the one (that)** I bought yesterday.*

Demonstrative pronoun
1. Antecedent: book
2. Gender & number: **Le livre** (*the book*) is masculine singular.
3. Selection: **celui**

Relative pronoun:
1. Function: *that* is the object of the relative clause.
(Answers the question: "I bought *what* yesterday?" *I* is the subject.)
2. Selection: **que**

Quel livre lisez-vous? **Celui** que j'ai acheté hier.

   masc. sing.   object

Which dresses do you prefer?
*I prefer **the ones (that)** are in front.*

Demonstrative pronoun
1. Antecedent: dresses
2. Gender & number: **Les robes** (*the dresses*) is feminine plural.
3. Selection: **celles**

Relative pronoun
1. Function: *that* is the subject of the relative clause.
(Answers the question: "*What* is in front?)
2. Selection: **qui**

Quelles robes préférez-vous? **Celles** qui sont devant.

   fem. pl.   subject

CELUI, CELLE TO SHOW POSSESSION

Demonstrative pronouns are also commonly used in a French structure to show possession (see **What is the Possessive?**, p. 24). For the same reason that "my father's house" can only be expressed in French by the structure "the house of my father," a similar French structure must be used to say the equivalent form "my father's." In this case, the word-for-word English translation of the French structure is "the one of my father." In French, *the one* agrees in gender and number with its antecedent, here "the house."

To choose the correct form, follow these steps:

1. Find the antecedent of *the one* or *the ones*.
2. Determine the gender and number of the antecedent.
3. Select the form of the demonstrative pronoun (see chart p. 182).
4. Add the preposition **de** (*of*).

Let us apply these rules to the following examples:

Which house are you selling? My father's.

the one of my father

1. Antecedent: house
2. Gender & number: **La maison** (*the house*) is feminine singular.
3. Selection: **celle**
4. Add **de**

Quelle maison vendez-vous? **Celle de** mon père.

fem. sing.

Which books are you reading? The young man's.

the ones of the young man

1. Antecedent: books
2. Gender & number: **Les livres** (*the books*) is masculine plural.
3. Selection: **ceux**
4. Add **de**

Quels livres lisez-vous? **Ceux du** jeune homme.

masc. pl.   de + le

Practice

In the following sentences:
 • Circle the demonstrative pronouns.

- Fill in the steps you would follow to choose the correct French form.
- Using the chart in this section, fill in the French demonstrative pronoun in the French sentences below.

1. She did not buy my house, but she did buy this one.

    1. Antecedent : _____

    2. Gender and number : feminine _____

    3. Demonstrative pronoun : _____

    4. **-ci** or **-là:** _____

Elle n'a pas acheté ma maison, mais elle a acheté _____ .

2. My courses are more interesting than those.

    1. Antecedent : _____

    2. Gender and number : masculine _____

    3. Demonstrative pronoun : _____

    4. **-ci** or **-là:** _____

Mes cours sont plus intéressants que _____ .

3. Lend me a blouse, please. This one.

    1. _____ : _____

    2. _____ : feminine _____

    3. _____ : _____

    4. _____ : _____

Prête-moi une blouse, s'il te plaît. _____ .

4. Which movie do you like? The one I saw with you.

Determine the demonstrative pronoun.

1. Antecedent : _____

2. Gender and number: masculine _____

3. Selection : _____

Determine the relative pronoun

1. Write the relative clause, adding the relative pronoun:

_____

2. Function of relative pronoun: _____

3. Selection : _____

Quel film aimez-vous? J'aime _____ _____ j'ai vu avec vous.

5. Which bakery do you go to? The one which is next to my house.

Determine the demonstrative pronoun

1. Antecedent : _____

2. Gender and number : feminine _____

3. Selection: _____

Determine the relative pronoun

1. Write the relative clause:

_____

2. Function of relative pronoun: _____

3. Selection : _____

A quelle boulangerie allez-vous? A _____ _____ est à côté de chez moi.

What is a Possessive Pronoun?

A **possessive pronoun** is a word that replaces a noun and indicates the possessor of that noun. Possessive comes from *possess,* to own.

Whose house is that? It's *mine.*

Mine is a pronoun that replaces the words *my house* and shows who possesses the house.

In English: Here is a list of the possessive pronouns:

SINGULAR
1st PERSON		mine
2nd PERSON		yours
	MASCULINE	⎧ his
3rd PERSON FEMININE		⎨ hers
		⎩ its

PLURAL
1st PERSON	ours
2nd PERSON	yours
3rd PERSON	theirs

Possessive pronouns never change their form, regardless of the thing possessed; they refer primarily to the possessor.

Is that your house? Yes, it is *mine.*
Are those your keys? Yes, they are *mine.*

The same possessive pronoun (*mine*) is used, although the objects possessed are different in number (*house* is singular, *keys* is plural).

John's car is blue. *His* is blue.
Mary's car is blue. *Hers* is blue.

Although the object possessed is the same (*car*), the possessive pronoun is different because the possessor is different (*John* masculine singular, *Mary* feminine singular).

In French: Like English, French possessive pronouns refer to the possessor. But unlike English, they must agree, like all French pronouns, in gender and number with their antecedent, that is, with the person or object possessed. In addition, the possessive pronoun is preceded by the definite article, which also agrees in gender and number with the object possessed. So there are masculine and feminine singular forms in both the singular and the plural.

The first letter of the possessive pronoun refers to the possessor and the ending of the possessive pronoun agrees with the noun possessed.

*Where are your books? **Mine** are in the living room.*

Possessor: *Mine* 1st pers. sing. = **m-**
Possessed: **Les livres** (*books*) is masculine plural = **les** + **-iens**

masc. pl. endings

Où sont vos livres? **Les miens** sont dans le salon.

1st pers. sing.
possessor

Here are the steps you should follow in choosing the correct possessive pronoun:

A. MINE, YOURS (**tu** form), HIS, HERS, ITS

In French, each of these possessive pronouns has four forms: 1) the masculine singular, 2) the feminine singular, 3) the masculine plural, and 4) the feminine plural.

1. Indicate the possessor. This will be shown by the first letter of the possessive pronoun.

mine	**m-**
yours	**t-**
(**tu** form)	
his	
hers	**s-**
its	

2. Establish the gender and number of the object possessed. Choose the definite article and the ending according to the gender and number of that noun.

- If the noun possessed is masculine singular, use the definite article **le** and add **-ien** to the first letter of the possessor.

>*Whose **book** is that?*
>A qui est ce **livre?**
>
>object possessed
>masc. sing.

>C'est **le mien.**   *It is **mine**.*
>C'est **le tien.**   *It is **yours**.*
>C'est **le sien.**   *It is **his/hers**.*

- If the noun possessed is feminine singular, use the definite article **la** and add **-ienne** to the first letter of the possessor.

>*Whose **house** is that?*
>A qui est cette **maison?**
>
>object possessed
>fem. sing.

>C'est **la mienne.** *It is **mine**.*
>C'est **la tienne.** *It is **yours**.*
>C'est **la sienne.** *It is **his/hers**.*

- If the noun possessed is masculine plural, use the definite article **les** and add **-iens** to the first letter of the possessor.

>*Whose **books** are those?*
>A qui sont ces **livres?**
>
>object possessed
>masc. pl.

>Ce sont **les miens.** *They are **mine**.*
>Ce sont **les tiens.** *They are **yours**.*
>Ce sont **les siens.** *They are **his/hers**.*

- If the noun possessed is feminine plural, use the definite article **les** and add **-iennes** to the first letter of the possessor.

> *Whose **magazines** are those?*
> A qui sont ces **revues?**
> |
> object possessed
> fem. pl.

Ce sont **les miennes.**   *They are **mine.***
Ce sont **les tiennes.**   *They are **yours.***
Ce sont **les siennes.**   *They are **his/hers.***

3. Select the proper form according to the two steps above.

Let us apply these two steps to the following examples.

> *She is reading her magazines. He is reading **yours.***
> 1. Possessor: **t-**
> 2. Noun possessed: **Les revues** (*the magazines*) is feminine plural.
> 3. Selection: **les + -iennes**

Elle lit ses revues. Il lit **les tiennes.**

> *Lend me your book. No, I'll lend you **hers.***
> 1. Possessor: **s-**
> 2. Noun possessed: **Le livre** (*the book*) is masculine singular.
> 3. Selection: **le + -ien**

Prêtez-moi votre livre. Non, je vous prêterai **le sien.**

B. OURS, YOURS (**vous** form), THEIRS

In French, each of these possessive pronouns has three forms: 1) the masculine singular, 2) the feminine singular, and 3) the plural (the same for both genders).

1. Indicate the possessor.

ours	nôtre
yours	vôtre
theirs	leur

2. Establish the gender and number of the noun possessed. Choose the definite article and the ending according to the gender and number of that noun.

   - If the noun possessed is masculine singular, use **le**.
   - If the noun possessed is feminine singular, use **la**.
   - If the noun possessed is plural, use **les** and add an "**-s**" to the possessor.

Let us apply these two steps to the following examples.

> *Whose house is it? It is **ours**.*

> 1. Possessor: **nôtre**
> 2. Noun possessed: **La maison** (*the house*) is feminine singular.
> 3. Selection: **la**

A qui est cette maison? C'est **la nôtre**.

*I will not lend you my magazines. I'll lend you **theirs**.*

> 1. Possessor: **leur**
> 2. Noun possessed: **Les revues** (*magazines*) is plural.
> 3. Selection: **les** + **-s**

Je ne vous prêterai pas mes revues. Je vous prêterai **les leurs**.

Here is a chart you can use as a reference.

	SINGULAR	PLURAL
mine	le mien la mienne	les miens les miennes
yours (**tu** form)	le tien la tienne	les tiens les tiennes
his, hers, its	le sien la sienne	les siens les siennes
ours	le nôtre la nôtre	les nôtres
yours (**vous** form)	le vôtre la vôtre	les vôtres
theirs	le leur la leur	les leurs

Practice

In the following sentences:
- Circle the possessive pronoun.
- Fill in the steps you would follow to choose the correct French form.
- Using the charts in this section, fill in the proper French possessive pronoun in the French sentences below.

1. I won't take his car. I'll take mine.

    1. Possessor: _____ -

    2. Object possessed: _____

    3. Gender and number : feminine _____

    4. Article and ending: _____ - _____

Je ne prendrai pas sa voiture. Je prendrai _____ .

2. I'm not going with my parents. I'm going with hers.

    1. Possessor: _____ -

    2. Object possessed: _____

    3. Gender and number: masculine _____

    4. Article and ending: _____ - _____

Je ne vais pas avec mes parents. Je vais avec _____ .

3. I'm not going with my parents. I'm going with his.

    1. _____ : _____ -

    2. _____ : _____

3. _____ : masculine _____

4. _____ : _____ - _____

Je ne vais pas avec mes parents. Je vais avec _____ .

4. Are you taking your book? No, I'm taking yours (familiar).

1. _____ : _____ -

2. _____ : _____

3. _____ : masculine _____

4. _____ : _____ - _____

Prends-tu ton livre? Non, je prends _____ .

5. Mary and Paul can read my notes, but I can't read theirs.

1. _____ : _____ -

2. _____ : _____

3. _____ : feminine _____

4. _____ : _____ - _____

Marie et Paul peuvent lire mes notes, mais je ne peux pas lire

_____ _____ .

What is a Relative Pronoun?

A **relative pronoun** is a word that serves two purposes:

1. As a pronoun it stands for a noun or another pronoun previously mentioned. The noun or pronoun referred to is called the **antecedent.**

> This is the boy *who* broke the window.
> antecedent

2. It introduces a **subordinate clause,** that is, a group of words having a subject and verb separate from the subject and verb of the main sentence. A subordinate clause cannot stand alone as a complete sentence.

> main clause   subordinate clause
> This is the boy *who broke the window.*
>   subject verb
>
> *Who broke the window* is not a complete sentence.

The above subordinate clause is also called a **relative clause** because it starts with a relative pronoun *who.* The relative clause gives us additional information about the antecedent *boy.*

In English: The selection of most relative pronouns depends on the function of the relative pronoun in the relative clause, and on whether the antecedent is a "Person" (this category includes human beings and live animals) or a "Thing" (this category includes objects and ideas). Sometimes, two different relative pronouns can be used to say the same thing. Here are the most common English relative pronouns:

A. SUBJECT OF THE RELATIVE CLAUSE

Refers to a person: *who*

> She is the only student *who* answered all the time.
> antecedent
>
> *Who* is the subject of *answered.*

Refers to a thing: *which*

> That movie *which* is so popular was in French.
> |
> antecedent
>
> *Which* is the subject of *is*.

Refers to a person or a thing: *that*

> She is the only student *that* answered all the time.
> |
> antecedent
>
> *That* is the subject of *answered*.

> This is the book *that* is so popular.
> |
> antecedent
>
> *That* is the subject of *is*.

As you can see, you sometimes have the choice between two relative pronouns; *who* and *that,* for instance.

B. DIRECT OBJECT OF THE RELATIVE CLAUSE

Although direct object relative pronouns are often omitted in English, we have indicated them in parentheses because they must be expressed in French.

Refers to a person: *whom*

> This is the student (*whom*) I saw yesterday.
> |
> antecedent
>
> *Whom* is the direct object of *saw*.
> (*I* is the subject of the relative clause.)

Refers to a thing: *which*

> This is the book (*which*) Paul bought.
> |
> antecedent
>
> *Which* is the direct object of *bought*.
> (*Paul* is the subject of the relative clause.)

Refers to a person or a thing: ***that***

> This is the student (*that*) I saw yesterday.
> |
> antecedent
>
> > *That* is the direct object of *saw*.
> > (*I* is the subject of the relative clause.)
>
> This is the book (*that*) Paul bought.
> |
> antecedent
>
> > *That* is the direct object of *bought*.
> > (*Paul* is the subject of the relative clause.)

C. INDIRECT OBJECT OR OBJECT OF A PREPOSITION IN THE RELATIVE CLAUSE

Refers to a person: ***whom***

> Here is the student I was speaking *to*.
> |
> antecedent

This English structure cannot be translated word-for-word into French for two reasons: 1. The French language does not permit dangling prepositions (see p. 145), and 2. the relative pronoun omitted in English must be expressed in French. To establish the French structure, you must restructure the English sentence, placing the preposition within the sentence and adding a relative pronoun. If you are not sure where to place the preposition and the relative pronoun, remember that they follow immediately after the antecedent.

SPOKEN ENGLISH	→	RESTRUCTURED
Here is the student		Here is the student
I was speaking *to*.		*to whom* I was speaking.

Whom is the indirect object of *was speaking*.

> Here is the student I was talking *about*.
> |
> antecedent

As in the case of the indirect object, spoken English often omits the relative pronoun and places the preposition at the end of the sentence. Again, you will have to restructure the sentence.

SPOKEN ENGLISH	→	RESTRUCTURED
Here is the student		Here is the student
I was speaking *about*.		*about whom* I was speaking.

Whom is the object of the preposition *about*.

Refers to a thing: *which*

Here is the museum he gave a painting *to*.
　　　　　　　|
　　　antecedent

SPOKEN ENGLISH	→	RESTRUCTURED
Here is the museum		Here is the museum
he gave the painting *to*.		*to which* he gave the painting.

Which is the indirect object of *gave*.

D. POSSESSIVE MODIFIER "WHOSE"

The possessive modifier *whose* is a relative pronoun which does not change its form regardless of its function or antecedent.

Find the woman *whose* car was stolen.
　　　　　|
　　antecedent

Whose is a possessive modifying *car*.

Look at the house *whose* roof burned.
　　　　　|
　　antecedent

Whose is a possessive modifying *roof*.

USE OF RELATIVE PRONOUNS

Relative clauses are very common. We use them in our everyday speech without giving much thought to why and how we construct them. The relative pronoun allows us to combine in a single sentence two thoughts which have a common element.

Let us look at a few examples to see how we construct relative clauses:

- Sentence A: The students passed the exam.
  Sentence B: They studied.

  1. Identify the element the two sentences have in common.

     The students and *they;* both words refer to the same persons. *The students* is the antecedent. *They* will be replaced by a relative pronoun.

  2. Establish the function of the relative pronoun in the relative clause. It will have the same function as the word it replaces.

     The relative pronoun will be the subject of *studied.* (*They* is the subject of *studied.*)

  3. Choose the relative pronoun according to whether its antecedent is a person or a thing.

     They refers to *students.* Therefore, its antecedent is a person.

  4. Select the relative pronoun.

     Who or *that* is the subject relative pronoun referring to a person.

  5. Place the relative pronoun after its antecedent.

     The students *who* studied passed the exam.
     or
     The students *that* studied passed the exam.
     antecedent   relative clause

- Sentence A: The French teacher is nice.
  Sentence B: I met her today.

  1. Common element: *the French teacher* and *her*
  2. Function of *her:* direct object
  3. Antecedent: *The French teacher* is a person.
  4. Selection: *whom* or *that*
  5. Placement: *whom* or *that* after *the French teacher*

  The French teacher, *whom* I met today, is nice.
  ⎣_____⎦   ⎣_____⎦
   antecedent   relative clause

In spoken English, you would say: "The French teacher I met today is nice." Notice that the relative pronoun *whom* is left out, making it difficult to identify the two clauses.

- Sentence A: Mary read the book.
  Sentence B: I was speaking about it.

  1. Common element: *book* and *it*
  2. Function of *it:* object of the preposition *about*
  3. Antecedent: *The book* is a thing.
  4. Selection: *which*
  5. Placement: *about which* after *the book*

  Mary read the book *about which* I was speaking.
  ⎣_____⎦   ⎣_____⎦
   antecedent   relative clause

In spoken English, you would say: "Mary read the book I was speaking about." Notice that the preposition is at the end and that there is no relative pronoun.

In French: Relative pronouns are used just as they are in English. The main difference is that, unlike English where the relative pronoun can sometimes be omitted at the beginning of a relative clause, the relative pronoun must always be expressed in a French sentence.

A. Subject of the Relative Clause

Refers to a person or a thing: **qui**

> *This is the student **who** answered.*
> |
> antecedent
>
> *Who* is the subject of *answered.*

Voici l'étudiant **qui** a répondu.

> *This is the book **which** is so interesting.*
> |
> antecedent
>
> *Which* is the subject of *is.*

Voici le livre **qui** est si intéressant.

Notice that **qui** is always followed by a verb.

B. Direct Object of the Relative Clause

Although these relative pronouns are often omitted in English, they must be expressed in French. Hence, we have indicated them in parentheses in the English sentences below.

Refers to a person or a thing: **que** (or **qu'** before a vowel)

> *This is the book **(which)** I bought.*
> |
> antecedent
>
> *Which* is the direct object of *bought.*
> *I* is the subject of the relative clause.

Voici le livre **que** j'ai acheté.

> *This is the student **(whom)** he saw.*
> |
> antecedent
>
> *Whom* is the direct object of *saw.*
> *He* is the subject of the relative clause.

Voici l'étudiant **qu'**il a vu.

Notice that **que** is always followed by a noun or pronoun.

The two following functions involve prepositions. Make sure that you work with the prepositions used in French and that you place the preposition within the sentence.

C. OBJECT OF THE PREPOSITION *DE* IN THE RELATIVE CLAUSE

Refers to a person: **de qui**

> *This is the man (that) I am speaking about.*
> |
>   antecedent

> You must restructure the dangling preposition.

SPOKEN ENGLISH	→	RESTRUCTURED
This is the man		This is the man
I am speaking *about*.		*about whom* I am speaking.

Voici l'homme **de qui** je parle.

Refers to a person or a thing: **dont**

> *This is the man (that) I am speaking about.*
>
> (see analysis above)

Voici l'homme **dont** je parle.

> *This is the book (that) I need.*
> |
>   antecedent

> Remember that *to need* is **avoir besoin de** (*to have need of*). Since we must work with the prepositions used in French, the relative pronoun is the object of the preposition **de:** "This is the book *of which* I have need."

Voici le livre **dont** j'ai besoin.

Refers to a person or a thing: **de** + **lequel**

Lequel must agree with the antecedent in gender and number. There are four forms of this relative pronoun.

	SINGULAR	PLURAL
MASCULINE	lequel	lesquels
FEMININE	laquelle	lesquelles

Also, the initial **le** and **les** of these pronouns function like definite articles when they follow **de** (i.e., **de** + **le** = **du** and **de** + **les** = **des**).

> *These are the books (**that**) I am talking about.*
> |
> antecedent

SPOKEN ENGLISH	→	RESTRUCTURED
These are the books		These are the books
I am talking *about*.		*about which* I am talking.

> Gender and number of antecedent: **Les livres** (*books*) is masculine plural.

Voici les livres **desquels** je parle.
> de + les
> masculine plural

D. OBJECT OF A PREPOSITION OTHER THAN *DE* IN THE RELATIVE CLAUSE

This section also covers indirect objects because relative pronouns are considered objects of the preposition **à** (see p. 151).

You will notice that there is more than one way to express the relative pronoun.

Refers to a person: preposition + **qui**

> *This is the man (**that**) I am thinking about.*
> |
> antecedent

SPOKEN ENGLISH   →   RESTRUCTURED
This is the man   This is the man
I am thinking *about*.   *about whom* I am thinking.

Remember that *to think about* is **penser à** in French.

Voici l'homme **à qui** je pense.

Refers to a person or a thing: preposition + **lequel**

Lequel must agree with the antecedent in gender and number. (See chart p. 204.) Also, following the preposition **à** (*to*) the initial **le** and **les** becomes **au-** and **aux-**.

*This is the man (**that**) I am thinking about.*

(See restructure above.)
Gender and number of antecedent: **L'homme** (*man*) is masculine singular.

Voici l'homme **auquel** je pense.

$$\boxed{\text{à + le}}$$
masc. sing.

*These are the pens (**that**) I write with.*

antecedent

SPOKEN ENGLISH   →   RESTRUCTURED
These are the pens   These are the pens
I write *with*.   *with which* I write.

Gender and number: **Les stylos** (*pens*) is masculine plural.

Voici les stylos **avec lesquels** j'écris.

masc. pl.

E. *DONT* = "WHOSE"

Dont is the French equivalent of the possessive modifier *whose*.

*This is the student **whose** mother came.*
Voici l'étudiant **dont** la mère est venue.

Here is a chart of French relative pronouns to which you can refer.

FUNCTION IN RELATIVE CLAUSE:	ANTECEDENT PERSON	THING
SUBJECT	qui	
DIRECT OBJECT	que	
OBJECT OF **de**	de qui dont de + lequel	dont de + lequel
OBJECT OF PREPOSITION (other than **de**)	prep. + qui prep. + lequel	prep. + lequel

To find the correct relative pronoun you must go through the following steps.

1. Find the relative clause. (You will have to restructure the English clause if there is a dangling preposition and add the relative pronoun if it has been omitted.)
2. Determine the function of the relative pronoun in the relative clause.
   • If the relative pronoun will be an object of a preposition in English, it will be the object of a preposition in French.
   • If the antecedent refers to a thing, you will have to determine its gender.
3. Select the French form from the chart above.

Let us apply the steps outlined above to the following sentences:

*The plane **that** comes from Paris is late.*

   1. Relative clause: that comes from Paris
   2. Function of *that:* subject of relative clause
   3. Selection: **qui**

L'avion **qui** arrive de Paris est en retard.

*Here are the books (**that**) I bought yesterday.*

1. Relative clause: that I bought yesterday
2. Function of *that:* direct object of relative clause
3. Selection: **que**

Voici les livres **que** j'ai achetés hier.

Notice the agreement of past participle **achetés** with the direct object **que** referring to **livres** (see p. 83).

*Where is the book (**that**) you need.*

1. Relative clause: that you need
2. Function of *that:* object of the preposition **de**
   Remember that *to need* is **avoir besoin de** (*to have need* **of**).
3. Type of antecedent: a thing (*book*)
4. Selection: **dont** or **duquel**

Où est le livre **dont** vous avez besoin.
Où est le livre **duquel** vous avez besoin.

de + lequel

*Where is the university (**that**) she is thinking about?*

SPOKEN ENGLISH	→	RESTRUCTURED
Where is the university she is thinking *about?*		Where is the university *about which* she is thinking?

1. Relative clause: about which she is thinking
2. Function of *which:* object of preposition **à**
   Remember that *to think about* is **penser à.**
3. Type of antecedent: a thing (*university*)
4. Gender of antecedent: **L'université** is feminine singular.
5. Selection: **laquelle**

Où est l'université **à laquelle** elle pense?

fem. sing.

*That is the boy (**that**) she is playing **with**.*

SPOKEN ENGLISH	→	RESTRUCTURED
That is the boy she is playing *with.*		That is the boy *with whom* she is playing.

1. Relative clause: with whom she is playing
2. Function of *whom:* object of preposition **avec**
3. Type of antecedent: a person (*boy*)

4. Gender of antecedent: **Le garçon** (*boy*) is masculine singular.
5. Selection: **qui** or **lequel**

Voici le garçon **avec qui** elle joue.
Voici le garçon **avec lequel** elle joue.

masc. sing.

Relative pronouns are tricky to handle and this handbook provides only a simple outline. Refer to your French textbook for additional rules.

RELATIVE PRONOUNS WITHOUT ANTECEDENTS

There are relative pronouns that do not refer to a specific noun or pronoun. Instead they refer to an antecedent which has not been expressed or to a whole idea.

In English: There are two relative pronouns that may be used without an antecedent.

What meaning *that which.*[1]

Here is *what* I read.

no antecedent

I don't know *what* happened.

no antecedent

It is easy to see that there is no antecedent, because antecedents (nouns or pronouns) come just before relative pronouns.

Which referring back to a whole idea, not to a specific noun or pronoun.

You speak many languages, *which* is an asset.

Antecedent of *which:* the fact that you speak many languages

---

[1]The relative pronoun *what* (meaning *that which*) should not be confused with other uses of *what;* as an interrogative pronoun (***What** do you want?* **Qu'est-ce que** vous voulez?, see p. 171), and as an interrogative adjective (***What** book do you want?* **Quel** livre voulez-vous?, see p. 127).

She didn't do well, *which* is a pity.

Antecedent of *which:* the fact that she didn't do well

In French: When a relative pronoun does not have a specific antecedent, the pronoun **ce** is added to function as the antecedent. It is followed by whatever relative pronoun would have been used if there had been a noun antecedent.

Let us apply these rules to the following examples:

*Here is **what** happened.*

1. Relative clause: what happened
2. Function of *what:* subject of *happened*
3. Selection : **qui**
4. No antecedent: add **ce**

Voici **ce qui** est arrivé.

*Show me **what** you bought.*

1. Relative clause: what you bought
2. Function of *what:* direct object of *bought*
3. Selection: **que**
4. No antecedent: add **ce**

Montrez-moi **ce que** vous avez acheté.

*I don't know **what** he is talking about.*

Restructure: *I don't know **about what** he is talking.*

1. Relative clause: about what he is talking
2. Function of *what:* object of preposition **de**
   Remember that *to talk about* is **parler de.**
3. Selection: **dont**
4. No antecedent: add **ce**

Je ne sais pas **ce dont** il parle.

*He doesn't speak French **which** will be a problem.*

1. Relative clause: which will be a problem
2. Function of *which:* subject
3. Selection: **qui**

4. No antecedent: add **ce**
(*Which* refers to the whole phrase "he doesn't speak French.")

Il ne parle pas français **ce qui** sera un problème.

*To speak French well, that's **what** I want.*

1. Relative clause: what I want
2. Function of *what:* direct object of *want*
3. Selection: **que**
4. No antecedent: add **ce**
(*What* refers to the whole phrase *to speak French well.*)

Bien parler français voilà **ce que** je veux.

Practice

I. In the following sentences:
- Underline the relative pronoun.
- Circle the antecedent.
- Identify the function of the relative pronoun by circling the appropriate identification: Subject (s), Direct object (do), Indirect object (io), Object of a preposition (op), or Possessive modifier (pm).

1. I received the letter that you sent me.   s   DO   IO   OP   PM

2. That is the woman who speaks French.   s   DO   IO   OP   PM

3. Here comes the man to whom I lent   s   DO   IO   OP   PM
money.

4. This is the book whose title I had   s   DO   IO   OP   PM
forgotten.

5. Paul is the student about whom I spoke.   s   DO   IO   OP   PM

II. Using a relative pronoun, combine the series of two sentences below into one sentence.
- Fill in the blanks showing the steps you have to follow.
- On the line below, write the combined sentence.

1. The girl is nice. She lives next door.

    1. Common elements: _____ / _____

    _____ is the antecedent.

    _____ will be replaced by a relative pronoun.

    2. Function of relative pronoun: _____

    3. Type of antecedent: _____

    4. Selection: _____

2. He spoke on a new topic. I knew nothing about it.

    1. Common elements: _____ / _____

    _____ is the antecedent.

    _____ will be replaced by a relative pronoun.

    2. Function of relative pronoun: _____

    3. Type of antecedent: _____

    4. Selection: _____

3. The new student is French. You are talking about her.

    1. Common elements: _____ / _____

    _____ is the antecedent.

    _____ will be replaced by a relative pronoun.

    2. Function of relative pronoun: _____

3. Type of antecedent: _____

4. Selection: _____

_____

_____

III. Find the French equivalent of the English relative pronoun in the following sentences.
- Fill in the blanks for each step you have to follow.
- Using the chart on p. 206, fill in the appropriate French relative pronoun.

1. The house that I am buying is expensive.

1. Relative clause: _____

2. Function of relative pronoun: _____

3. Selection: _____

La maison _____ j'achète est chère.

2. The student who is sleeping works at night.

1. Relative clause: _____

2. _____ of relative pronoun: _____

3. Selection: _____

L'étudiant _____ dort travaille la nuit.

3. This is the book I was talking about.

1. Restructured: _____

_____

2. Relative clause: _____

3. _____ of relative pronoun: _____

Remember *to speak about* is **parler de.**

4. Selection: _____ or _____

Voici le livre _____ je parlais.

4. I liked the girls I went on a trip with.

    1. _____ : _____

    _____

    2. Relative clause: _____

    3. Function of relative pronoun: _____

    4. Selection: _____ or _____

J'ai aimé les filles avec _____ je suis allé en voyage.

Answer Key

What is a Noun? 1. boy, classroom, teacher 2. Smiths, France, ship 3. textbook, painting, cover 4. Mary, Evans, Paris, class 5. temperature, classroom 6. lion, children 7. truth, fiction 8. kindness, understanding, world 9. honesty, policy 10. teacher, explanations, children

What is Meant by Gender? I. 1. masculine 2. ? 3. feminine 4. masculine 5. ? 6. feminine 7. ? II. 1. feminine 2. feminine 3. masculine 4. masculine 5. feminine

What is Meant by Number? The first letter corresponds to Column A, the second to Column B. 1. P P 2. P ? 3. S S 4. P P 5. P ? 6. S S 7. S S 8. P P 9. P P 10. S S

What are Articles? 1. les 2. l' 3. des 4. une 5. de l' 6. la 7. un 8. du 9. le 10. de la

What is a Mute "h"? 1. l' 2. la 3. l' 4. le (The dictionary entry is always singular. Some words end in "s" in the singular; *héros* is one of those words.) 5. l'

What is the Possessive? 1. the parents of some children 2. the color of the dress 3. the entrance of the school 4. the speed of a car 5. the covers of the books

What is a Verb? 1. purchase 2. were 3. enjoyed, preferred 4. ate, finished, went 5. realized, dreamt 6. felt, seems 7. stayed, expected 8. was, see, struggle, get out 9. attended, celebrate 10. increases, remains

What is an Infinitive? I. 1. write 2. swim 3. be 4. speak 5. have 6. teach II. 1. to do 2. study 3. to learn 4. leave 5. to travel

What are Auxiliary Verbs? I. 1. did 2. will 3. do 4. - (*avoir- to have*-is an auxiliary verb) II. Auxiliary *être:* aller, revenir, tomber. Auxiliary *avoir:* avoir, être, manger, acheter III. 1. sont (d) 2. voilà (b) 3. est (c) 4. il y a (a) 5. il y a (a)

What is a Subject? 1. Q: What rang? A: The bell. Q: Who ran out? A: The children. 2. Q: Who took the order? A: One waiter. Q: Who brought the food? A: Another. 3. Q: Who voted? A: The first-year students (*or* The students). 4. Q: What assumes? A: That. Q: Who is right? A: I. 5. Q: What is? A: It. Q: What is a beautiful language? A: French

What is a Pronoun? The antecedent is in parentheses. 1. she (Mary), him (Peter) 2. they (coat, dress) 3. herself (Mary) 4. We (Paul, I) 5. it (bed)

What is a Subject Pronoun? I. 1. I, *je* 2. they, *ils* or *elles* 3. you, *tu* 4. we, *nous* 5. you, *vous* 6. he, she, or it, *il* or *elle* II. 1. je 2. vous 3. nous 4. tu 5. elles 6. vous 7. vous 8. ils

What is a Verb Conjugation? I. STEM: fin- ENDINGS: -*is*, -*is*, - *it*, -*issons*, -*issez*, -*issent* CHOISIR: chois**is**, chois**is**, chois**it**, chois**issons**, chois**issez**, chois**issent**. II. STEM: répond- ENDINGS: -*s*, -*s*, -, -*ons*, -*ez*, -*ent* VENDRE: je vend**s**, tu vend**s**, il vend, nous vend**ons**, vous vend ez, ils vend**ent**

What are Affirmative and Negative Sentences? I. 1. We do not (don't) want to speak English in class. 2. He did not (didn't) do his homework yesterday. 3. Helen was not (wasn't) home this morning. 4. Paul cannot (can't) go to the restaurant with us. 5. Paul and Mary did not (didn't) drive to Paris. II. 1. do not 2. did not 3. not 4. -not 5. did not III. 1. want 2. do 3. was 4. can 5. drive

What are Declarative and Interrogative Sentences? I. 1. Did Paul and Mary study all evening? 2. Does his brother eat a lot? 3. Do the girl's parents speak French? II. 1. did 2. does 3. do III. *Est-ce que* would precede: my mother and father went to the movies. *N'est-ce pas* would follow: my mother and father went to the movies. 1. noun subject, mother and father 2. verb, went 3. pronoun, they = *ils*

What is Meant by Mood? 1. verbs 2. indicative (3. 4. and 5. can be in any order) 3. present 4. past 5. future 6. imperative 7. subjunctive 8. conditional

What is Meant by Tense? 1. time 2. simple 3. two 4. auxiliary 5. main 6. & 7. present, past 8. simple 9. conditional (or future) 10. simple

What is the Present Tense? I. 1. reads 2. is reading 3. does read II. 2. lit 3. lit

What is the Imperative? I. 1. Study every evening. 2. Let's go to the movies once a week. II. 1. Don't sleep in class. 2. Let's not speak in class. III. 1. P 2. I 3. P 4. I 5. I

What is a Participle? I. 1. -ing 2. present 3. past 4. past 5. present II. 1. am speaking 2. were studying 3. are bringing 4. will be trying 5. None (The present participle, "singing," is used as an adjective describing "canary.")

What is the Past Tense? I. (The answers to 1. and 2. can be inverted.) 1. imparfait 2. passé composé 3. imparfait 4. passé composé 5. avoir 6. être 7. present 8. past participle II. 1. auxiliary 2. être 3. subject 4. avoir 5. direct object 6. verb III. 1. went out, was going = imparfait 2. were doing = imparfait 3. called = passé composé 4. was talking = imparfait, saw = passé composé 5. prepared = passé composé

What is the Past Perfect? 1. (-1), (-2); 2. (-1), (-1), (-2); 3. (-1), (-2). The verbs marked (-2) take the *plus-que-parfait*.

What is the Future Tense? I. 1. will study, study 2. 'll do, do 3. will travel, travel 4. will attend, attend II. 1. A. present, future B. future, future 2. A. future, present B. future, future

What is the Future Perfect? 1. (2), (1) 2. (1), (2). The verbs marked (1) take the *futur antérieur;* the verbs marked (2) take the future.

What is the Conditional? 1. PC, I 2. PP, PPC 3. PC 4. I, I 5. PC 6. F, P

What is a Reflexive Verb? I. 1. themselves 2. herself 3. yourself 4. yourselves 5. themselves II. 1. se 2. nous 3. me 4. te 5. vous 6. se

What is Meant by Active and Passive Voice? I. 1. cow, cow, A 2. bill, parents, P 3. bank, bank, A 4. everyone, everyone, A 5. spring break, all, P II. 1. are taking, P, The final exam is taken by all the students. 2. brought, PP, The children were brought to the park by the teacher. 3. will read, F, That article will be read by people all over the world.

What is an Adjective? 1. noun 2. pronoun 3. descriptive 4. possessive 5. interrogative 6. demonstrative 7. gender 8. number

What is a Descriptive Adjective? The noun or pronoun described is between parentheses. 1. young (man), French (newspaper) 2. pretty (she), red (dress) 3. interesting (it) 4. old (piano), good (music) 5. tired (Paul), long (walk)

What is a Possessive Adjective? I. The noun described is between parentheses. 1. my (exam) 2. your (house) 3. our (mother) 4. your (clothes) 5. his (boots), her (gloves), their (walk) II. A. 1. possessor, *m-, t-, s-* 2. gender a) masculine, feminine, *-on;* feminine, *-a* b) *-es* B. 1. notre, votre, leur 2. nos, vos, leurs

What is an Interrogative Adjective? I. The noun modified is between parentheses. 1. which (class) 2. what (exercises) 3. which (hotel) 4. which (restaurant) II. 1. which, dresses, *quelles* 2. what, trade, *quel*

What is a Demonstrative Adjective? I. The noun modified is between parentheses. 1. that (restaurant) 2. this (test) 3. those (books) 4. these (houses) (*Those* is a demonstrative pronoun, see p. 182. It does not modify a noun, it replaces it.) II. 1. that, singular, *cette* 2. this, singular, *cet* (The "h" is mute, see p. 21.) 3. these, plural, *ces*

What is Meant by Comparison of Adjectives? I. 1. The teacher is older than the students. 2. He is less intelligent than I am. 3. Mary is as tall as Paul. 4. That boy is the worst in the school. 5. Paul is a better student than Mary. II. 1. composition 2. exercises 3. girl 4. student

What is an Adverb? The word modified is between parentheses. 1. early (arrived) 2. really (quickly), quickly (learned) 3. too (tired) 4. reasonably (secure) 5. well (speaks), very (well)

What is a Conjunction? (The words to be circled are in **bold**; the words to be underlined are in *italics*.) 1. *Mary* **and** *Paul* were going to study *French* **or** *Spanish*. 2. *She did not study* **because** *she was too tired*. 3. *Not only had he forgotten his ticket*, **but** *he had forgotten his passport as well*. 4. *She knew he was mean*, **yet** *she still loved him*. 5. *They borrowed money* **so** *they could go to France*.

What is a Preposition? I. 1. about 2. from 3. around 4. contrary to 5. between II. 1. I know about what he was speaking. 2. To whom are you explaining the grammar? 3. For whom are you making the dress?

What are Objects? 1. Q: The children took what? A: A shower. DO 2. Q: They ate what? A: The meal. DO Q: They ate with what? A: Pleasure. OP 3. Q: He sent what? A: A present. DO Q: He sent a present to whom? A: His brother. IO 4. Q: They paid for what? A: The books. OP Q: They paid with what? A: A credit card. OP

What is an Object Pronoun? I. 1. it, DO 2. him, OP 3. it, OP 4. me, DO 5. us, IO 6. you, IO II. 1. her, direct object, *la* 2. it, direct object, book, *le* 3. them, indirect object, persons, *leur* 4. them, indirect object (in French), type of antecedent, *y* 5. her, object of preposition, *elle* 6. them, object of preposition, no, Robert and Paul, masculine, *eux* 7. me, disjunctive, *moi* 8. them, object of preposition, Is it the object of the preposition *de* (*of*), thing, *en*

What is an Interrogative Pronoun? I. 1. who, subject, person, *qui* 2. who, object of preposition, person, *qui* 3. what, function of pronoun, object of preposition, type of antecedent, thing, *quoi* 4. who, function of pronoun, direct object, type of antecedent, person, *qui* 5. what, function of pronoun, direct object, type of antecedent, thing, *que* II. 1. skirts, singular (the question asks: which one), *laquelle* 2. antecedent, books, gender, number, plural (the question asks: which ones), *lesquels* 3. antecedent, sisters, gender, feminine, number, singular, *laquelle*

What is a Demonstrative Pronoun? I. 1. this one, house, singular, *celle, -ci, celle-ci* 2. those, courses, plural, *ceux, -là, ceux-là* 3. this one, antecedent, blouse; gender and number, singular, demonstrative pronoun, *celle, -ci or -là, -ci, celle-ci* 4. the one, movie, singular, *celui, that* I saw with you, direct object, *que, celui que* 5. the one, bakery, singular, *celle,* which is next to my house, subject, *qui, celle qui*

What is a Possessive Pronoun? 1. mine, *m-,* car, singular, *la -ienne, la mienne* 2. hers, *s-,* parents, plural, *les -iens, les siens* 3. his, possessor, *s-,* object possessed, parents, gender and number, plural, article and ending, *les -iens, les siens* 4. yours, possessor, *t-,* object possessed, book, gender and number, singular, article and ending, *le -ien, le tien* 5. theirs, possessor, *leur,* object possessed, notes, gender and number, plural, article and ending, *les -s, les leurs*

What is a Relative Pronoun? I. The antecedent is between parentheses. 1. that (letter), direct object 2. who (woman), subject 3. whom (man), indirect object 4. whose (book), possessive modifier 5. whom (student), object of preposition II. 1. girl/she, girl, she, subject, person, who, The girl who lives next door is nice. (Don't forget that the relative pronoun must be placed right after its antecedent.) 2. topic/it, topic, it, object of preposition, thing, which, He spoke on a new topic about which I knew nothing. 3. student/her, student, her, object of preposition, person, whom, The new student about whom you are talking is French. III. 1. that I am buying, direct object, *que, que* 2. who is sleeping, function, subject, *qui, qui* 3. This is the book about which I was talking, about which I was talking, function, object of preposition, *dont* or *duquel* (the antecedent *book* = *le livre* is masculine; therefore, *de* + *lequel* = *duquel*), dont/ duquel 4. Restructured, I liked the girls with whom I went on a trip, with whom I went on a trip, object of preposition, preposition + *qui* or preposition + *lequel, avec qui, avec lesquelles* (the antecedent *filles* is feminine plural)

Index